SURRENDERED
HEART

How God's Calling Shapes Relationships

RICK ALLEN

Published by StoryBuilders Press

Hardcover: 979-8-89833-019-4
Paperback: 979-8-89833-020-0
eBook: 979-8-89833-018-7
Audiobook: 979-8-89833-021-7

This book is dedicated to Dr. David Topazian, Dr. Dan Fountain, Dr. David Thompson, Dr. Bruce Steffes, Dr. Bruce Dalman, Dr. John Crouch, and Dr. David Stevens for their obedience to our Lord. Their vision, hard work, and dogged determination has changed the trajectory of global healthcare missions.

———————————

"We stand on the shoulders of the faithful."

TABLE OF CONTENTS

CHAPTER 1

CALLED, BROKEN, SURRENDERED

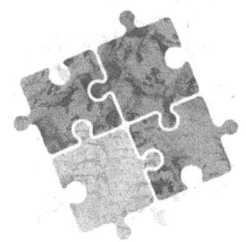

I was a pastor for eight years, and it nearly destroyed my marriage. I know that's probably not the first thing you expected to read when you picked up this book. Here's the backstory.

In 2007 I took on the role of pastor for a small congregation struggling to recover from a devastating church split. Sadly, in the church fracture a number of people were harmed—not physically, but their emotional and spiritual health was significantly impacted. I thought I knew what I was stepping into. I had served as an elder at my previous (much larger and healthier) church.

I had led missions committees. I had been in other leadership positions. I believed I understood ministry challenges.

I didn't.

I had been around the frays of spiritual battle, but I hadn't truly been *in* the battle until I stepped into this pastoral role. It was extremely disruptive to me personally and to my relationship with my wife, Linda.

Ministry of any kind can be hard on a marriage, and quite frankly, Linda and I were nowhere near prepared for what we were entering. The pressures were unlike anything I had experienced. We did not anticipate how it would affect us personally and as a couple.

As we stepped into this wounded and broken church, the spiritual battle there revealed our own brokenness. Nearly my entire life of faith, God has been impressing on me the concept of full surrender. Time and time again, God has asked me, "Do you trust Me?"

Sometimes the answer has been a confident yes. More often it has been a peeling back of layer after layer of control.

After building a successful career in business, the 9/11 attacks in 2001 upended every solid thing I had built. Through a series of events—including a dramatic dream in which I realized I did not, in fact, fully trust God—I began to step out in faith. I began to surrender control of my life and my future.

I never imagined I would pastor a church. After all, business was my area of experience and expertise. But after a season of prayer and uncertainty about what was next, it seemed like one more act of surrender when someone asked me to lead this struggling congregation. It was one more way to trust God with my life.

I gave up a twenty-five-year-long successful business career with all the trappings of worldly success to pursue ministry.

It was scary, but I stepped into the calling with excitement and conviction. Though the pain in the church was deep, I felt energized by the possibility of making a real difference.

I quickly became immersed in church policies, interpersonal disagreements, music wars, and every other difficult thing you can think of. Yes, there were times of despair when I sometimes questioned if I was doing more harm than good, but mostly I felt like I was fulfilling my calling. God had given me this role, and I would see it through.

Meanwhile, Linda stepped into a position that forced her to operate out of her greatest weaknesses even as I was operating in my areas of strength.

I loved my calling. She hated it.

Linda is an introvert who cherishes privacy. Being the pastor's wife in a small church meant that everyone knew our business. She felt constantly scrutinized, measured, and never free. She did not sign up for that level of exposure, and she did not thrive in it.

I wish I had protected her more. I wish I had been willing to flex my calling to safeguard our marriage. Eventually, I did resign my position, but not before our marriage had paid a heavy price.

As I watched Linda withdraw more and more under the never-ending scrutiny, it became clear that my calling could not come at the expense of her well-being. That realization was the beginning of my wrestling with God over whether to stay or leave.

I will say it out loud: Following God's calling is not easy. Sometimes a calling comes with a clear course of action. But more often, the path is not linear or simple. And as I found out while serving as a pastor, God's calling impacts every area of our lives, including the relationships with those we are closest to.

At the highest level, our relationship with God has to come first, then the relationships with our spouse and family, and finally our relationships with ministry partners and those we serve. How do we best honor God's calling when it comes to each of those relationships? Again, I'll be the first to say that it's not easy, and I haven't always gotten it right. Relationships require an intentional willingness to surrender for the sake of love and unity. And sometimes that even means surrendering your own calling, which seems unthinkable.

Even though I knew Linda was struggling, for a time I pushed ahead. The work at the church was important, and God had called me to it. I was not interested in the kind of surrender that felt like failing or quitting. I know now that surrendering for the benefit of those you love is not weakness; it's a reflection of Christ's humility. But without humility guided by the Holy Spirit, it was easy for me to slip into the mindset that my calling superseded everything else.

Every one of us is broken. Every one of us is sinful. But those things get manifested when you step out in faith, when you step forward in obedience and say, "Here I am, God. Use me." That's when Satan wakes up.

And that's what happened to Linda and me. The enemy of our very souls found a way to exploit our individual brokenness and then exploit the relational weaknesses between the two of us.

The spiritual battle was real. It was personal. And it left scars.

PEOPLE ARE COMPLICATED

Relationships can be messy. You don't have to travel to the other side of the world to know that. A glance in the mirror or a conversation around your own kitchen table will do. We think differently. We come from different backgrounds. We carry different expectations. Even in the healthiest contexts, relationships take work. Every marriage requires adjustment.

Every family has its own dynamics to navigate. Every workplace and friendship bring relational challenges.

My story with Linda is just one example of how relationships can be tested when you follow God's call. And while our struggle happened in the context of pastoral ministry, those serving cross-culturally as healthcare missionaries face the same challenges—and often greater ones.

In my current role as CEO of MedSend, an international medical missions organization, I get to see God at work every day. I've traveled to many countries. I've seen God's hand move in and through people all around the globe in remote village clinics, crowded hospitals, and makeshift surgery tents.

I've had every emotion you can imagine. Some stories bring me to my knees in worship. Others move me to tears. I am continually in awe of what God is doing. And I am equally moved by the courageous and faithful men and women He has called to do it. Medical professionals who love God and are deeply committed to His call bring hope and healing to a world that desperately needs both. They are people who have trained for years, prayed through difficult decisions, uprooted their families, and stepped into places few are willing to go. Their stories are remarkable.

It's easy to focus on the highlights—lifesaving surgeries, breakthrough care for women and babies, community transformation, groundbreaking national training programs, and spiritual renewal. But I also see the other side. I see the high cost that healthcare missionaries pay, and it breaks my heart. They give up the prestige, comfort, and financial security that a medical career in the United States might afford them. But beyond those obvious sacrifices, there is a quieter, heavier toll. They often pay a steep price in their relationships.

The work of a medical professional is by nature intense. It's physically exhausting and emotionally demanding. Every day involves holding other people's health and often their very lives in your hands. Now take that already stressful profession and place it in a high-pressure, low-resource environment. Add inadequate equipment, limited medications, a shortage of trained colleagues, and a patient load that never ends. Then add a layer of political instability, security threats, cultural isolation, and separation from extended family.

It is a recipe for chronic, cumulative stress.

Missionary healthcare workers face situations that would be unthinkable in a US hospital. One of our MedSend grant recipient physicians recently told me that during a malaria outbreak in his community, they lost sixty children per month. That's two children dying every day.

There is no way that someone who's never lived through that kind of loss can understand what it means to a person's heart and soul. We simply can't fathom it. Committed, faithful followers of Christ find themselves asking unanswerable questions.

Why did this person have to die?
Could I have saved them if I'd had the right resources?
Why does God allow so much suffering?
Did I make a mistake responding to God's call?

And the relentless pace means there's no time to grieve, little margin for processing, and no space to rest. For many, even the thought of stepping away for a break feels impossible because if they do, someone might die. If they go on vacation or spend time with family, even more may die.

And every night when they finally return home from the hospital or clinic, they are often emotionally empty. Spouses and children can feel invisible in the shadow of the work. Missionary kids (MKs) especially can feel the strain. They often blindly accept their missional role as part of the family. They, like their parents, are unprepared. And when they encounter trauma or abuse, there's often a self-inflicted code of silence so they don't bring shame to the family. And unfortunately, once an issue or challenge is uncovered, there are limited resources to fully address the impact on the child's life.

In any family, the condition of the children is directly related to the condition of the parents. If a marriage is not doing well or if the parents are under enormous stress at work—incredible working hours, unrealistic demands, and a lot of death—the whole family suffers.

Beyond the family strain, there's also the potential for difficulty with coworkers—fellow missionaries or national counterparts. With a few exceptions (you'll read about one later in the book), missionaries don't get to pick their coworkers. Mission teams are often made up of people from different denominations and family backgrounds. Though they all love God and share a similar vision, it doesn't mean they'll naturally click. Physical proximity does not equal relational closeness.

It shouldn't come as a surprise that different personalities and ideas of how things should be done can create friction. And when you're living in close quarters and making big decisions under stress, often in life-and-death situations, even small disagreements can feel like big ones. Being on the same team doesn't always mean you're instantly compatible.

The same thing can happen with national coworkers. Local staff bring cultural insights and language skills, which are incredible gifts. But they undoubtedly have different ways of approaching patient care and various timelines for doing so. What feels urgent to a Western-trained doctor might be seen differently in the local culture. And deeply rooted traditions about authority, communication, and how resources are used can easily lead to misunderstandings.

Everyone may want the same outcome—to show Christ's love and offer the best care possible—but it takes real patience and humility to work through those differences. On the surface, tensions may look like matters of personality, preference, or culture, but they are often the very fault lines where spiritual attack takes place.

A SPIRITUAL BATTLE

As I said, serving as a healthcare missionary is demanding. It is stressful. Many enter that calling with expectations far removed from the reality they encounter once they arrive. They feel the strain on their marriages, within their families, among their coworkers, and even in their walk with God Himself.

Relational breakdown, more than lack of skill or funding, is one of the leading causes of medical missionaries leaving the field. Whether it's a faltering marriage, struggling children, or a crumbling community, relational strain can make the work unsustainable. And over time, the cost of the calling becomes too great to bear.

Many healthcare missionaries have carried their calling for decades, feeling God's leading toward international service since middle school or high school. They've worked hard, excelled academically, and completed years of medical school and residency, all toward the goal of serving God as a missionary doctor. Then, after all those years of preparation and sacrifice, they arrive on the field and face the reality that they must compromise—even surrender.

They must submit to a spouse's needs, the dynamics of a team, or the culture where they now live. That kind of surrender requires deep faith and self-discipline. They must trust that yielding to others will not erase or diminish their calling. Instead, it becomes a way of living out the call of God in a way that honors Him, their marriage, and the people He has put on their path. And sometimes God even asks them to surrender their own personal calling.

I understand this deeply because I've lived it. I wrestled and fought with God for months before resigning my pastoral role. Stepping into that calling had already required an enormous amount of faith, and then, when I'd given so much, I had a hard time accepting that God would ask me to step out. That was a different kind of surrender. I found myself asking, "Is this obedience or defeat?"

Sometimes God calls you to walk away from something even when your heart is still deeply attached, and that kind of surrender can be agonizing. I loved the people I served, and I had invested so much of my life in them. But over and over again in the Christian life, God asks, "Will you hand this to Me? Will you trust Me with it?"

MedSend-supported healthcare missionaries are on the front lines of a global spiritual battle. These incredible families see things, hear things, and experience things that will change their lives forever. When one spouse is thriving in ministry but their partner is withering under the weight of it, when coworkers don't see eye to eye, when cultural differences create painful misunderstandings, Satan seizes the opportunity. He exploits individual weaknesses and then relational weaknesses, driving painful wedges where unity should be.

And yet God redeems. God heals. God restores.

MY HOPE FOR THIS BOOK

The stories you will read in this book are not tidy. They are not struggle-free. Some are not even fully resolved yet. A few of the people you will meet have requested that we change their names, either to protect sensitive ministry locations or in acknowledgment that their story is unavoidably intertwined with others' stories. They were open-hearted and vulnerable in their sharing while at the same time acutely aware that each person has only their own perspective.

Though it is difficult to capture the entirety of a life of ministry in just one chapter, you will see that these stories are saturated with God's presence in the midst of the hard things. The men, women, and children you will meet on these pages are a testimony to how God's calling transforms relationships.

In their pain, God draws near. In their surrender, God meets them.

- In Suja and Tom's story, you'll see how God asks for our hearts before our service.

- In Troy and Rebekah's story, you'll see God's faithfulness even as seasons change.

- In Luke and Kate's story, you'll see how God cares for the refugee.

- In David and Joy's story, you'll experience the freedom that comes from doing what you're called to do, not more or less.

- In Seth and Rebecca's story, you'll see how God sustains even in the pain of lament.

- In Dan and Heather's story, you'll see how calling can change to meet a family's needs.

- In Justin and Olivia's story, you'll learn the blessing that comes with waiting on God's timing.

- In Stephanie and Andrew's story, you'll learn the importance of building a strong support team.

- In Michelle and Adam's story, you'll see what happens when you trust God to reconcile what you cannot fix on your own.

- In Eric and Rachel's story, you'll see how relationships are the mission.

- In Christina and Greg's story, you'll see what it looks like to finish well.

- In Omega and Julie's story, you'll see how lasting ministry starts with a strong, unified home.

God's calling is ultimately meant to bring wholeness, flourishing, and peace—shalom. But because we live in a broken world, it often brings conflict and strain before it brings maturity. Sometimes God's call strains relationships to the point of breaking. Sometimes it forges something stronger than what existed before.

In all circumstances, God is faithful. He is the One who sustains.

"Now may the God of peace himself sanctify you completely, and may your whole spirit and soul and body be kept blameless at the coming of our Lord Jesus Christ. He who calls you is faithful; he will surely do it" (1 Thessalonians 5:23–24).

If you are preparing to go to the mission field, I hope this book will give you eyes to see what's ahead—not to scare you but to equip you. In your eagerness to get started, don't neglect the relational aspect of your preparations. Have conversations with your spouse. Engage your children. Talk with your sending agency about how they will support you when the pressure builds.

If you are already on the field, I want you to know you are not alone. The struggles you face in your relationships are not a sign of failure. As you'll see as you read the coming chapters, they are common, even predictable. Reach out. Seek help. Invest in your own health and your family's health.

If you are a missions supporter, my hope is that you will understand the deep relational cost of healthcare missions and how your generosity can play a part in sustaining not only the work but the workers themselves.

And be sure to pray. Pray for strength. Pray for resilience. Pray for God's unique calling to shape your relationships in the way that only He can.

CHAPTER 2

WHEN SERVING BECOMES LORD OF YOUR LIFE

SUJA AND TOM BRANE

S uja Brane was exhausted. In fact, she was burning out but didn't realize it. For the last three years, she had worked at a remote women's and children's mission hospital in Mali. But the area had become a high-risk zone due to political upheaval, expat kidnappings, and growing security threats from Al-Qaeda and ISIS. Eventually, her mission agency told her it was time to go. In fact, the agency told the whole team to go because their presence had become more of a liability than a lifeline.

But to Suja and her husband, Tom, leaving felt like a betrayal to the people of Mali. They knew they were evacuating during the country's time of greatest need for help. Leaving went against the grain of everything they had trained for and prayed about.

In the end, they found themselves moving westward to Senegal. Tom had made the decision to move there because he was going to serve alongside the Beer-Sheba Project, a Christian development farm. Unfortunately, that left Suja stranded in her mission with no hospital to join, no team to support, and no plan. For someone who had spent her entire life in pursuit of medical missions, this felt like an unraveling of purpose.

As Suja wrapped up leaving Mali, her life on full throttle, God impressed on her heart a question. It was as if He put His hand on her shoulder and asked, "Suja, what are you doing?"

Caught off guard by such a question, she replied in her mind, *Lord, what do You mean 'What am I doing?' I am serving You!*

In her stillness, she pressed further into prayer, confused and lost, and sought the Lord. Then she sensed Him ask, "Suja, who is Lord of your life?"

Offended, she responded, "How can You ask me such a question? You know that You alone are Lord of my life."

And then God convicted her with this thought: "Suja, am I Lord of your life, or is *serving Me* lord of your life?

With that, Suja was left speechless and humbled. At first, she tried to fight it and work around it. Serving God was good. Sacrificing her time and energy was noble—even admirable.

But to her surprise, as they moved to Senegal, God sidelined her. For nine months, she stopped. She had no clinic and no title, just grief and prayer and the ache of unspent purpose.

God made it clear that stewarding her body, her mind, her marriage, and her family were just as important to Him as using her talents for Him. For years, Suja had poured out her life in the name of ministry, but aspects of her offering had stopped being fragrant to the Lord as the collateral damage caused by her drive to serve Him became foul-smelling. That broke her servant's heart.

In that season of waiting and stillness, something changed. Suja's view of what it meant to serve came to a head as she sat at God's feet.

A LONG SEASON OF PREPARATION

Tom Brane was a small-town boy from northern Indiana. Suja grew up in Cincinnati, Ohio, a first-generation Indian American from a close-knit family. On paper, they might have looked mismatched, but when they met at Cincinnati Bible College as nineteen-year-olds, something just clicked.

Tom was studying youth ministry, and Suja had come to take a year of Bible classes before diving into her pre-med track at the University of Cincinnati. Their first connection was friendship, but over time, that friendship began to change shape. Tom knew when Suja's year was over that she'd pursue her pre-med studies elsewhere, and he didn't want to lose her. He realized what he felt for her was more than just friendship, and a courtship began. By the end of Suja's first year of med school, they were married.

They had both been drawn to missions from a young age. And now began a long season of preparation. Eleven years would pass before they ever boarded a plane to serve overseas. In that time, Suja finished med school and residency while Tom served as a youth minister for a few years, followed by teaching in a small Christian school. They had three children in six years. Suja began working in family medicine at a private practice in Cincinnati.

They waited patiently to get their bearings in their marriage and as parents. Their lives looked pretty normal during that stretch—steady jobs, church community, and birthday parties. But underneath it all, a sense of readiness was building. They always knew they weren't staying in the United States, and a nicer house or a better job were never their goal. Their goal was obedience. They wanted to go wherever the Lord called them.

At a global health conference in Louisville, Kentucky, everything finally crystallized for them. They put their house up for sale and joined a mission agency. Just a short while later, they got on a plane with their six-year-old, four-year-old, and three-month-old children. Leaving was bittersweet, but they were unified in why they were going.

What they didn't know—what they *couldn't* know—was how much the journey would cost them.

LOVING LIFE IN AFRICA

After spending a year in France learning French, Tom and Suja arrived in Burkina Faso in 2013, jet-lagged and wide-eyed with three small children and a decade of preparation behind them. Every sacrifice, conversation, and postponed desire had led to this.

The agency told them to spend the first year in the country learning language and culture. They obeyed, listened, and practiced. Internally, they both tried to locate their purpose on the ground, joining ministries and helping several patients navigate the public healthcare system. From the outside, they looked like missionaries, but the truth was, they were just doing their best to adjust.

By God's blessing, their children grew to love life in Africa. Their new home had a perfect climbing tree in the backyard. Tom and Suja grew their proficiency in French, and God blessed them with an excellent homeschool teacher named Minta for their children. Minta followed them on all their missionary adventures, even across borders. With a stable answer to quality education, their life overseas began to take shape.

They served in Burkina Faso for four years. Tom started income-generating activities, teaching individuals how to start a kettle corn and moringa soap business. He saw the need for and importance of agricultural development, which sparked an interest in a resource called Farming God's Way.

Tom had spent years supporting Suja during medical training. This time, Suja played a supportive role so the family could integrate themselves well into a new culture. They connected with neighbors, learned to eat out of a communal bowl, and navigated the market. They found ways to contribute relationally and spiritually. They forged friendships with their community and learned to shed pieces of their Americanness as they gained greater cultural awareness.

Suja struggled to find her place medically in Burkina Faso because there were no medical ministries in the city where they lived and very few in the country. Eventually, she learned there was a mission hospital that served women and children just four hours away in the neighboring country of Mali. It seemed the perfect opportunity to use her gifts as a family medicine doctor to their full extent.

Leaving Burkina Faso was harder than expected. The whole family had grown attached to both the people and the place, but Suja was ready to fulfill God's specific purpose for her life. So they packed up and moved to their next chapter.

BRINGING A SQUIRT GUN TO A FOREST FIRE

Once in Mali and after another year of language immersion, Suja got involved serving at the 181-bed mission hospital. She was one of eight medical missionaries who shared medical responsibilities. Two of them were doctors, and Suja was the only female on the team who was married with kids. She found she was as driven as ever to pour out her life to worship the Lord as He was worthy of excellence.

Tom knew that coming to Mali meant there was no set ministry for him to join, so he sought one out. There were agricultural programs to grow and discipleship relationships to invest in. He took advantage of identifying needs in the community and worked to meet them. It was meaningful and quiet work but much less urgent and less defined than his work in Burkina Faso had been. Unlike Suja's call, there was no daily crisis pulling him out of bed in the morning.

Their roles in ministry had always supported the greater mission of serving God. The challenge in this season was that both Tom and Suja were involved in separate full-time ministries. As time went on, the pace of their lives began to diverge. They were both still committed to and unified with each other, but the weight distribution of their work began to tilt in one direction—Suja's.

Suja quickly realized the overwhelming challenge of balancing caring for a family in a rural context and caring for her patients in a resource-limited environment. Most of her patients had medical diagnoses that were way beyond her scope of practice or knowledge, which led to countless hours of research about how best to treat them.

Suja threw everything she had into the hospital, and even when she was home, she wasn't. Her mind was still at work going over patient charts, and she couldn't let it go. She didn't know how to stop, and the work began to consume her. Even in their supposed off hours, Suja pulled out her laptop, responded to emails, and wrote referral letters while her kids watched a movie.

Caring for the home and the family was also a full-time job. Everything took effort and forethought. The Mali dust in the air constantly settled over everything in the house. Meals had to be made from scratch, and the family was forced to buy certain ingredients such as cheese, milk, and boneless chicken breast in the capital city five hours away.

The kids were a high priority too. Suja poured herself into their schooling and social needs, doing her best to make sure they had what they needed—fun birthday parties, meaningful social interactions in their limited context, quality engaging education, help with homework and studying as needed, and tasty American meals despite living in the middle of nowhere.

Suja loved being both a mom and a wife, but balancing the demands of home and ministry was becoming increasingly unmanageable. She quickly became very aware of how blessed her male colleagues were to have a spouse whose primary role was managing the home and caring for the children. That support at home enabled them to pour themselves into their medical ministries. They were available to carry a heavier workload and respond to emergencies.

Because Tom was busy developing his ministry, he had limited time to help with household responsibilities. Since Suja did not have that type of support system at home, it began to take a toll on their marriage. They were both pouring themselves into ministries, but the bulk of the household responsibilities fell on Suja's shoulders. It was not sustainable—not in a healthy way that didn't inflict collateral damage on other areas of their life.

Tom could see that his wife was exhausted, and he admired her dedication. Suja made sure the family's physical needs were met and worked hard to keep all the plates in her life spinning. But in doing so, they had to make a sacrifice. They began to disconnect on sharing home responsibilities and aligning priorities.

In Suja's view, there were natural expectations that fell on her as the mother, whether Tom wanted to help or not. She was the one who remembered that the kids needed new shoes for school, knew their sizes, and ordered them when it was time. When they needed help with their homework, they reached out to Suja. When it was time to celebrate a birthday in the family, it was Suja who planned it.

Suja and Tom still worked as a parenting team, pouring into the children, spiritually nurturing their faith, and developing a strong God-honoring character in them. They were able to meet those challenges, but in his lowest of lows, Tom grappled with the ongoing demands and sacrifices that came with being married to a medical missionary. He loved Suja and fully supported her, but this life of service had revealed itself as a path paved with quiet resentment, unmet expectations, and personal cost.

SIDELINED

In 2020, Suja and Tom realized that while their marriage was still intact, it wasn't in the healthiest place. The truth was that Suja wasn't really okay. She was physically worn down, and the emotional distance between her and Tom was deeper than she allowed herself to admit. Deep down, they both believed that God had more in store for their relationship and that He was calling them to something deeper and more connected. But Suja didn't know how to reconcile the needs of her patients with the needs of her family, so she just kept soldiering on in her duties.

Meanwhile, the external pressures were mounting. The region was becoming more unstable by the week. Expats were being kidnapped, and foreigners were being targeted. Living under the threats of being kidnapped by Al-Qaeda or ISIS was a daunting risk, especially with children at home. Suja felt as if the Lord had invited them to grow in their faith, trust, and dependence on Him, but pushing through fears about security added another layer of stress in Suja's life.

It was around that time that without even realizing it, Suja's serving may have taken the place of lordship in her life. She was juggling more than she could possibly handle, and true to her pattern, she responded to the stress by working even harder. It drove her deeper into a cycle she couldn't break—pushing herself harder while her mental and emotional health quietly wore thin.

She was balancing being a mom and a doctor by putting in late nights and working on weekends. Her brain was always on overdrive. It could not rest. She developed insomnia, and her body learned how to function on four hours of sleep a night. Living at a high level of stress became the unhealthy new normal for her.

Then in mid-2020, their sending organization decided that all missionaries would be evacuated by the following spring. The security threat was simply too great, and everyone would need to leave by April 2021.

The news landed like a blow. Suja had poured herself into her patients and the community. And now at the moment of deepest need, she would be pulled out. Regardless of their feelings, she and Tom obeyed the directive and packed up their home, grieving all they were losing. Mali had fulfilled Suja's conviction to serve the Lord, but at a high cost.

Senegal offered a landing place. It was a safer country, and they would be working with a familiar organization. Tom joined the Beer-Sheba Development Farm where he could equip local farmers and also minister to the locals about the Master Farmer, God. The kids were able to continue homeschooling and found a community with new friends. They were happy to be out of the danger zone of Mali.

But there was no plan, no mission strategy, no clinic, and no team there that needed Suja's expertise. There was no medical work for her—not now, not yet, maybe not at all.

She had been extracted from the most intense, immersive work of her life and dropped into a holding pattern. It was like God had benched her when the game was still going. There were no patients, no staff, and no emergencies to solve.

There was just time, silence, and God. In that quiet with all her routines and busyness stripped away, the questions began to press in. Suja heard it, not in an audible voice but in the weight of conviction from God.

"Suja, am *I* your Lord or is *serving Me* your lord?"

The words sliced straight through her carefully built theology of sacrifice and worship. She had spent her entire adult life doing things for God—good things, hard things, urgent things. But now it became painfully clear that serving had become her god.

She fought it at first. She offered to serve in small ways, but every door remained shut.

God wasn't asking her to pivot; He was asking her to stop.

As Suja prayed in her stillness, a new conviction began to unfurl in her heart. She reflected deeply on her worship. *Was her offering fragrant to the Lord, or was it foul? If what she was doing was no longer a fragrant act of worship, then why?*

Obedience and worship had always driven Suja. But with this conviction in her heart, she realized that the collateral damage of her offering was not pleasing to the Lord. She made it her mission to figure out how to address that. She wanted to pour her life out for His honor and glory. If the way she was doing it was not fulfilling that, then something had to change.

A SEASON MEANT TO HEAL

Burnout isn't always obvious. Suja had gone so long surviving on momentum that when the brakes finally slammed, she realized she didn't know how to live any other way.

But God is a provider.

At just the right moment, Suja attended a retreat that focused on debriefing and processing the experiences and challenges medical missionaries face. There she found a safe space to recognize and verbalize what was going on internally, and that week became the start of something transformative for her. She began to address her difficulty balancing her medical missionary work and home life.

Right after that, God blessed her with the MedSend Longevity Project, a multifaceted initiative that provides professional, relational, and spiritual support to healthcare missionaries. It covered the cost of counseling with a trauma-informed counselor who was familiar with the conditions of mission life. That began the deep, soul-level excavation that Suja needed.

With her counselor's support, she picked through the internal structures she had built over the years of high-functioning exhaustion—the difficulty of differentiating between laziness and rest, especially if rest was done for a prolonged period of time, and the idea that anything less than full-throttled sacrifice was just spiritual compromise.

One session at a time, God started rewiring Suja's understanding of obedience and service. And she came back again and again to one

Bible verse: "My grace is sufficient for you, for my power is made perfect in weakness" (2 Corinthians 12:9). *Weakness*—not strength, not output, not productivity—was where she found grace. She was meant to live in partnership with the Lord. And for the first time in her adult life, Suja began to understand it and embrace it.

With time, Suja eased back into medicine cautiously and intentionally. She was asked to assist the nurses at the small clinic on the farm where Tom worked. When nurses were struggling with complex patient needs, Suja slowly stepped in while setting boundaries that she'd never set before.

This time, she aspired to build her work around her personal capacity, not the need. She made it a goal to turn off her phone and strived to work from a place of rest. She didn't always accomplish that, but she intended to pour herself out for the Lord in a healthier way. Her medical work sometimes caused her to cross boundaries she had drawn, but she became more aware of the dangers of doing so. She began to keep a much closer eye on her own pulse, the pulse of her marriage, and the pulse of her family. This time, she tried to steward her talents, body, mind, marriage, and family well.

Of course, she didn't transform immediately. She still lived in the tension of balancing pressing demands with rest. But now she was aware of the pitfalls she could fall into and had a richer understanding of what God meant when He said, "Follow Me."

For the first time in years, Tom saw the Suja he had fallen in love with reappear. He never asked her to stop being who she was, but he had missed her in their marriage and their unity. Their restoration season began with more time for one another and more counseling. Trust wasn't rebuilt overnight, but their willingness to try was enough to keep going one more day, every day.

Suja started asking better questions. Instead of "Can I make a difference?" she asked, "What is God asking me to do in this patient's life?" She had once thought of herself as someone built for crisis—strong, capable, durable. But now she saw the deeper truth: God had never asked her to burn out for Him; He had asked her to abide in Him.

The kids noticed. Tom noticed. Even Suja noticed. She was more present and rested than before—not always productive, but alive in a different way. It didn't make the past disappear, and it didn't fix everything, but it marked the beginning of a new way forward.

A PLEASING AROMA

Today, Suja still lives in the tension of having a God-honoring ministry-life balance. She is busier now than she ever was in Mali and has more pressure and responsibilities on her shoulders. She knows it is easy to slip into old habits. Because of that, she has to make daily decisions and seek discernment from the Lord in order to balance service, rest, and family. Though she is considerably better than her condition a few years ago, she doesn't always get it right. But with God's grace and with grace for herself, she keeps trying.

Their children, who were small when they left for their first mission, have grown up on the field. And that didn't just mean new cultures, languages, and transitions. It meant parents who were often stretched thin or went back to work after dinner. Throughout the years, the Branes gave a lot to missions, to their community, and to the patients. And now, as their children step into adulthood, Tom and Suja are discerning what it means to have intentional family presence and give to their children.

At the time of this writing, their oldest daughter, Anna, is at Purdue University navigating the complexities of American college life. Their second daughter, Naomi, is finishing high school. Their youngest, Josiah, just turned fourteen and enjoys anything sports-related and the outdoors.

The questions Suja and Tom ask now are different than they used to be.

What does faithful parenting look like in the eighteen- to twenty-four-year-old stage of our children's lives?

How can we intentionally and wisely support our college-aged children spiritually, physically, emotionally, and financially while still serving on the field?

The answers that Tom and Suja have for those questions will shape their next steps as missionaries. There are still unknowns in the new season ahead, but they're not afraid of the next chapter. They move forward now at a unified pace.

Looking back on the season of being sidelined, Suja knows that while it is important to steward her talents well for the Lord, it is just as important that she steward her body, mind, marriage, and family in a way that honors Him. Relying on God's power in her weakness was a difficult mindset shift, but it was instrumental in helping her approach her medical ministry in a healthier, more sustainable way.

God's grace is indeed sufficient, even when it doesn't feel that way. And serving from a posture of weakness allows God's power to be displayed more fully. What Tom and Suja have to offer has become fragrant again. This time, the aroma rises not from work, pride, and exhaustion but from humility, unity, and surrender.

And it is pleasing, not just to each other and their children but to the One who asked for their hearts all along.

MY TAKE: SURRENDER YOUR SERVICE

The story of Suja and Tom Brane touches something deep and personal in me. Their experience mirrors much of what my wife and I have walked through both in ministry and in marriage. When Suja recounts hearing the Lord ask, "Am I your Lord or is *serving* Me your lord?" I was brought to a full stop. That question is a piercing challenge to the soul.

The temptation to make service our identity is dangerously subtle, especially for those who feel called to high-impact work. It's easy to convince ourselves that we are sacrificing for the Lord when in truth we may be serving out of pride, ego, or a desire to justify our worth. I've done it. Many of us have. When service rather than Christ Himself becomes the centerpiece, even our best efforts can become distorted.

I believe the Branes' story holds deep encouragement. There is grace in the slowing. There is healing in the stopping. There is redemption in the rebuilding. If any part of their journey resonates with you—if you're running on fumes or you're unsure whether it's obedience or pride driving your pace—I encourage you to stop. Seek counsel. Ask the hard questions. And most importantly, bring your whole heart back before the Lord. He doesn't need your service; He wants your surrender.

CHAPTER 3

GOD'S CALLING AND GOD'S TIMING

TROY AND REBEKAH SAMMONS

Rebekah Sammons stared at the photo on her husband's phone. It was just a tree—not a tree *near* something, not a tree *in front of or behind* something. It was just a tree standing in the dust with a lonely little water pump beside it.

Her husband, Troy, clearly unbothered by the lack of roads or any other sign of civilization, gave her an excited smile. He'd had that mission-high after returning from his second scouting trip to South Sudan.

"This is where the town is," he said.

She blinked. "I'm sorry. *Where* exactly is the town?"

He zoomed in on the water pump. "Right there."

Rebekah's marriage to Troy had come with several surprises—interaction with cows on a daily basis, machete maintenance in the living room, and dreams that involved moving to far corners of the world. But South Sudan felt like a whole different kind of stretch for their family. There were no maps that led to this spot. There were no stores, no schools, and not even a gas station—just that lonesome tree.

Okay, Rebekah thought. *So I'm going to bring our four babies to that tree. And what? Just hope it all works out?*

To be fair, Troy saw something she didn't. He saw a potential mission base, a cattle project, and a wellspring of gospel opportunity. He could see men gathered under that tree, watering their herds and also hearing about Jesus. He saw purpose in the dust; Rebekah just saw dust.

That moment standing over Troy's phone became a kind of shorthand for how ministry callings were revealed in their relationship. They were never mismatched in purpose; it was more like they were differently timed. Troy was quick to say yes. Rebekah was slower and more intentional, especially when tiny humans were involved. And there were so many tiny humans. Four kids will test anyone's sense of adventure.

In the end, though, Troy knew instinctively that the tree held promise. But he could see it wasn't the right time or place for his family.

This give-and-take rhythm wasn't new. After fifteen years of serving on the mission field, Troy and Rebekah had learned to wait for clarity together. They had learned to trust that God's timing and answer would eventually come, and with it unity in their calling.

THE SAME PLACE AT THE SAME TIME

Rebekah had grown up in a mission-minded church. At a young age, she learned what it meant to be a missionary, and her family supported missionaries from the get-go. By high school, she was going on short-term mission trips to Romania and Africa. Those experiences clarified that she wanted to raise a family on the field, and she began to pray for a husband with a similar calling. Her desire was, yes, to chase adventure and help others, but ultimately she wanted to obey God's plan for her life. She didn't know when or where, but she knew she wanted her life's work to count for the Kingdom.

Troy grew up in California with animals, adventure, and a fierce streak of independence. He came to faith early and wholeheartedly. When he committed to something, he went all in—a trait that continued throughout his life.

Veterinary medicine was his dream, but missions kept finding him. At nineteen, he went on a trip to Cameroon with a veterinarian who used working with cattle as a means to reach local tribes. Troy watched that man slip through cultural barriers with nothing more than a stethoscope and a cow halter, and something clicked. *This was it.* This was how he could serve: through livestock as the common language.

Troy came home from that trip changed. He pursued veterinary school and focused on intercultural studies and animal science. He could see his future on the field. His call was shaping up.

Troy and Rebekah had met years earlier when Troy and Rebekah's brother were college roommates. But they had no thought of a relationship at that time because little sister Rebekah was only thirteen years old. But now, Rebekah was a college student herself, planning for a year-long mission trip. Rebekah's brother reintroduced them by emailing Troy a copy of Rebekah's prayer postcard along with a not-so-subtle nudge about how she might be "a good match." It was part fundraising and part matchmaking. Troy eventually reached out with interest to meet up with her.

Their relationship unfolded long distance through emails, calls, letters, and visits. He traveled; she traveled. When they eventually got engaged, it wasn't because things lined up neatly. Rather it was because they believed in the same calling, even if they weren't necessarily using the same road to get there. They shared a vision: serve God, raise a family, go wherever He sends them. What they didn't share—yet—was the same sense of pace.

Troy was ready to go—like go *now*. His plan was to finish veterinary training and move directly to the field. Rebekah also wanted to go, but she knew herself. She needed time, and she wanted to start their marriage with some semblance of stability. They also had some serious student loans to figure out how to pay back. So they made a plan: Work for a couple of years, learn about veterinary practice, save, get donor support, and then launch—preferably to Kenya, a country they were both familiar with. It sounded great on paper, but life doesn't usually follow paper plans.

Not long after their wedding, Rebekah found herself holding a positive pregnancy test. And not long after that, there was another one. The childhood vision she had—being a missionary with a family—was starting to feel heavier than she'd imagined. She knew she wanted to do the work as a mom, but she didn't realize how it would actually feel *being* a mom on the field.

Suddenly, the certainty of God's calling on their lives was met with the uncertainty of God's timing.

BABY BAGS AND SUITCASES

Rebekah was already deep in baby world, a mother of two and newly pregnant with a third, when Troy squeezed in an exploratory trip to Kenya without her and the kids. He thought it would help confirm their vision to become full-time missionaries. Instead, it did the opposite.

Troy was placed in the slums for part of his stay with no running water, unreliable electricity, and stenches from the nearby sewer that seeped under the doorframe. It was by no means a curated mission trip with a designated guesthouse and a mosquito net draped over fresh sheets. This was the real deal.

And everyone was sick. Troy's teammates on the field were sick. The kids on their team were sick. Every day, someone had either a stomach bug, a fever, or something worse. When Troy relayed the reality of the situation, all Rebekah could think about was her unborn baby. She was terrified to take a newborn there.

Rebekah had memories of being a short-term missionary in a slum earlier in her life, and the idea of living with cockroaches running out from under the fridge door made her sick to her stomach. Meanwhile, Troy was on fire. He loved the trip—the people, the dirt, the chickens on the roads, the energy of it all. To him, cockroaches weren't a deal-breaker; they were a rite of passage. He came alive in Kenya.

Though Troy didn't dismiss Rebekah's discomfort about a potential move, he didn't quite understand the depth of it either. Tension began to build between them and hum in the background of their conversations. It was like a radio trying to play two different songs at the same time. Troy was moving at one life tempo, and Rebekah was moving at another.

Once Troy got back from this exploratory trip, it became a sore topic. When he talked about going back to Kenya full-time,

Rebekah's body tightened. She wasn't saying no, but she couldn't get herself to say yes either, not with the memory of the sickness and dirtiness of the slum so sharp in her mind. Fears of their babies catching something that no one could pronounce gave her a helpless feeling.

She still believed in their shared vision, but the idea of dragging toddlers and babies into that environment felt reckless and maybe even prideful or selfish. *Hadn't God given them these kids? Weren't they just as much a ministry?*

Troy wrestled too—not with the call itself but with the delay. Every day that passed felt like another step away from the dream they'd named together. He understood the stakes, but part of him felt like he was losing time. He'd prayed for these doors to swing open, and he was eager to finally walk through them.

Eventually, they united under the plan they had already set in motion all those years ago. By the time they packed up—baby bags and suitcases—Rebekah was six months pregnant with their third child and had two toddlers in tow. They landed in Kenya with high hopes.

SEPARATE LIVES UNDER ONE ROOF

Troy and Rebekah's first placement was at a children's organization. Troy dove into the work with all the passion he'd saved up over the years—caring for animals, fixing fences, building relationships, and teaching the local children. It was everything he'd dreamed of.

But Rebekah was stranded—not metaphorically but physically. The housing was nearly a mile away from the main ministry center, and she had no car and no easy way to engage with anyone. So she stayed home with the kids while Troy disappeared into his work. It was hard for Rebekah not to feel the distance. She began to be lonely and overwhelmed with motherhood. She wondered how the vision that had once set her heart on fire had somehow turned into taking care of crying babies in a developing country full of dust and mosquitos.

Troy came home excited, full of stories of men he'd prayed with, kids he'd served, and projects underway. Between the veterinary work and the local kids' ministry, his days filled up fast. There were fences to fix, volunteers to coordinate, boys who needed mentorship, and cows—always cows. His workload left him physically exhausted and emotionally full. This was what he had trained for. He was doing what he had dreamed of, and it was good work.

Most days, Rebekah couldn't see it the way Troy did because she wasn't there. She was home chasing toddlers, trying to figure out dinner with unfamiliar and limited ingredients, and nursing an infant while the power flickered on and off. She tried to match Troy's energy, but inside she was slipping. She felt disappointed in herself for not being stronger, disappointed in the dream for not matching her vision, and disappointed in the rhythm of their life that felt so lonely. They were the only missionaries at the orphanage, so it was really isolating.

Though neither of them said it out loud, a distance between them began to grow. Their vision hadn't died, but for Rebekah, it was beginning to fade. They didn't have a daily ministry together other than Rebekah supporting Troy by asking him how his day had been. They were still under the same roof, but the call that had once pulled them forward together was pulling them at different speeds.

And yet they stayed.

And the babies began to grow up. The tension didn't magically disappear, but neither did their commitment to keep walking forward toward the shared vision, even if one was sprinting toward it and the other was still catching her breath.

A NEW RHYTHM IN SOUTH SUDAN

At the end of their first mission term, Troy and Rebekah began working with a new group that brought aid to infants in need of rescue. During this season, they adopted a son, bringing their family to six. With a new family member and in search of new opportunities for ministry, Troy and Rebekah began to seek out the Lord's next steps.

In God's divine timing, another missionary family reached out and asked them to pray about joining their efforts in Sudan. Troy committed to the exploratory trip that produced the photograph of the lone tree and the water pump. Knowing what such a remote and harsh environment would do to his family, he wisely turned down that opportunity.

But that didn't mean they said no to Sudan entirely.

Instead, Troy felt an instant conviction about the influence of livestock. He realized that in South Sudan, if you could "talk cow," doors opened. Language barriers didn't matter so much when someone knew how to diagnose hoof rot or help a cow deliver a calf in the middle of the night. Cows were the common language and the currency of trust. In fact, cows mattered more than almost anything. They were symbols of identity, pride, power, and money. Troy learned that a man might be quicker to care for his bull than his wife due to a deeply ingrained belief that cows were irreplaceable—women not so much.

If Troy showed up as a vet and part of a church team, there would be a natural bridge. The men could trust him because Troy cared for what they cared about most, and that trust would extend to the church. In other words, the fields would be ripe for the harvest. South Sudan would be the perfect place for their ministry.

Rebekah also saw this vision clearly, and with Troy willing to find a place for them to live that had an actual town, she was ready to say yes. But if Kenya had been the warm-up, South Sudan was the main event.

Because of the hardship of living in a place like that, missionaries to the area were told to expect to live three months on the field and then take one month off. The Sammonses' family rhythm became a rotating door of adjustments. They'd arrive, settle in, push through the heat and dust, and then leave just long enough to almost recover before heading back. It was a constant cycle of effort and exhaustion.

For Troy, the work was worth it. Every week brought new stories and new relationships with real spiritual traction. He was living his calling in a place tailor-made for his gifts. Rebekah didn't complain, but there were signs of mounting pressure with this lifestyle, especially with the kids getting caught in the undertow.

The children were school-aged by then, bouncing between locations, curricula, and time zones. Rebekah homeschooled as best she could, but the inconsistency wore on everyone. What once had felt like a sacrifice for the Lord began to feel like surrender to a pace and pressure that her soul couldn't sustain in the long term. They tried to adapt and adjust their expectations, but after a few years of this routine, Rebekah's body and heart signaled that she was burning out.

Eventually, they had to make a change. They knew their children in high school needed more than what homeschooling in those circumstances could provide. So Troy and Rebekah made the difficult choice to enroll the two oldest kids in a boarding school in Kenya. They didn't make the decision lightly; they wrestled, prayed, debated, and wept. They never imagined that part of the cost of ministry would be watching their kids pack their suitcases.

Despite finding an educational solution for the kids, Rebekah still felt like she was handing over a piece of her heart and hoping someone else knew how to hold it. She knew the school was safe, even excellent, but it felt like a calling was going unanswered if they were not directly discipling their own children. Could their family continue to sustain this pace of life, or was God revealing to them a different tempo?

They had to face the questions: What was their ministry now? Was this season of parenthood the right timing for what they had envisioned as bright-eyed college students? Or had the vision shifted over the last decade of mission work and family growth?

After six years in Sudan, they came to the conclusion that God's timing was just as important as God's calling.

A DETOUR IS JUST ANOTHER ROAD AFTER ALL

Leaving Sudan wasn't a clean break. They didn't necessarily have confidence or a ten-point, next-step plan. They just knew something had to change.

So the Sammonses moved back to Kenya near the boarding school where their two older children were enrolled. At first, the relocation was purely practical. It made more sense to be near their children rather than keep trying to live fragmented lives across borders. The goal was stability and space to breathe.

What they didn't expect was that in this seemingly in-between place, they would start to move toward their calling at the same pace once again.

They started out as dorm parents and held that role for two years. Rebekah helped students navigate transitions and homesickness, bringing her full self into the emotional rhythms of community life. After so many years of diapers and dishes in isolation, a sense of missional purpose filled her days again. It was the first time she had something of her own ministry, contributing in a way that mattered outside the walls of their home.

Troy's shift was more complicated. After being a dorm parent, he moved into a regional managerial role and half-time chaplaincy at the school, shepherding students and preaching in chapel. It was good work, but it didn't quite scratch the itch that South Sudan had stirred in him. He missed the directness of the stripped-down, life-or-death nature of preaching the gospel in a barren place that had nothing else to lean on. It felt like a detour from the veterinary side of things. Still, he showed up, and over time he stopped seeing it as a detour and embraced it as this season's road.

What they both had to learn is something that no mission training or pre-field counseling can ever quite prepare you for. Sometimes the hardest part of ministry isn't the hardship itself but the disorientation that follows. Often there's a moment when the vision starts to blur and you're left asking, "What now?"

But even in that disorientation, Troy and Rebekah found grace with one another. They began having better conversations that were raw and honest. Rebekah said that's what held them together through fifteen years on the field. Maybe even more than the calling, it was their commitment to stay in the conversation.

That rhythm of talking and listening became the compass for their family. They moved multiple times, made major decisions, and delivered some hard yeses and harder nos, but one pattern always repeated: Rarely were they called to the same thing at the same time. Fortunately, they learned that God doesn't waste that tension and is ready for heart work when people ask for it.

Troy calls it yielding—letting one person move forward when the other isn't quite ready, or vice versa. He learned that obedience doesn't have to be simultaneous in order to be sincere. He knew that rushing a decision never works, so he surrendered their timeline to God. Their story became one of adjusting again and again, and learning how to walk together even if the road split or one of them was sprinting and the other one needed to sit down and rest.

As of this writing, Troy and Rebekah are still in Kenya. Rebekah continues her work at the school, deeply invested in the students and staff. Troy has stepped into a regional leadership role supporting teams, developing young leaders, and mentoring men with both theological depth and practical tools. The vet in him hasn't gone anywhere; it's just woven now into the broader fabric of their ministry.

The kids are older. Some are preparing to launch on their own, and two are still at home. The days of babies and homeschooling are behind them, but the lessons from that season remain. Their story is still unfolding, and they don't know exactly what's next. But that's okay.

They've stopped chasing the ideal chapter and are living the one God keeps writing, detours and all. They've discovered that the real ministry wasn't just in the cows; it was in the long season of slow obedience.

And in all that, they've come to understand these truths: God's calling is always constant, and His timing is always patient.

MY TAKE: YIELDING IN OBEDIENCE

I love Troy's use of the word *yielding*. It captures the reality of two people deeply called to serve but also navigating the tension between calling, marriage, and family. Troy and Rebekah had to learn to yield to each other, to the circumstances, and ultimately to God's leading.

Yielding is not easy. I'll admit (and my wife would agree) that I'm more of a steamroller by nature. But Troy and Rebekah's experience is a beautiful reminder that obedience sometimes means knowing when it's time for your spouse to flourish, even if it means adjusting your own dreams.

That dynamic of yielding applies in a marriage and cascades through every level of ministry. First, we submit to God, then to our spouse, then to our teammates and partners, and finally to the people we're serving.

It takes a deep willingness to surrender. Love and obedience require flexibility. One of the hardest lessons in missions is realizing that your personal sense of calling, even if it's been decades in the making, must sometimes yield to the needs of others. That's especially difficult when you've sacrificed so much to get there in the first place. But true obedience trusts that surrendering for the sake of others doesn't erase your calling; it refines it.

Today, Troy and Rebekah are serving in ways that don't quite look the way they once imagined. But maybe that's an illustration of a deeper truth in their story—that God honors daily yielding and slow, steady obedience.

CHAPTER 4

BECOMING THE REFUGEE

L U K E   A N D   K A T E   M I T C H E L L

The clinic stood still and quiet in the sticky Myanmar heat, fans whirring overhead as Luke and Kate moved through the halls. The power was spotty again, flickering every few minutes. They didn't talk much as they packed up their supplies for what was supposed to be a routine trip out of the country to renew a visa.

But outside, the atmosphere on the streets was tense. The military had tightened its grip, and since the coup in 2021, everything had begun to unravel. Schools were shuttered, civil servants had vanished, and entire towns were bombed.

By 2023, foreign workers were being watched, and some were being arrested.

Luke checked the local clinic's medicine cabinet one last time while Kate dusted off the metal-framed bed where they'd delivered so many babies. Everything in the room seemed to hum with memories.

The clinic had become both a refuge and a risk. During the COVID pandemic and the military uprising, their medical facility had been the only one operating in a region of 800,000 people. It had stayed open even when all the hospitals around them closed. But now, its existence and theirs felt dangerously visible.

As they walked out that day, they thought they would be back in a week. They left with just three days' worth of clothes. Unfortunately, the eruption of war closed the doors for them to return.

The sad thing was that there was no intelligence being shared with the community. There had always just been a feeling that the governmental situation was not normal—Myanmar being Myanmar. The Mitchells didn't realize at the time that once they left, they would not be allowed to go back.

When they prayed about their abrupt departure, it was as though God told them, "It's not your turn to serve right now."

So they were left without a home or a mission field, kicking and screaming as they clung to memories of the Myanmar they could no longer return to. Without a new post or assignment, the only place they could go was back to their hometown in the United States. The last time they visited Texas, they were on furlough. This time, they were coming back as evacuees.

Back in the States, they landed hard—physically and spiritually. The speed of Western life, the shocking ease of buying groceries, and the irrelevance of small talk made it feel like they were on a different planet. People asked casual questions about their experience: "How was it out there?" "What's next for you?"

But Luke and Kate Mitchell had no answers that didn't sound like grief.

In Scripture, the faithful are often referred to as pilgrims, strangers, exiles, or the remnant. The Bible has much to say about what the Israelites experienced as exiles in Babylon, but still, no one tells you how much it hurts to be displaced.

Though the door to the clinic in Myanmar was locked behind the Mitchells, in their hearts it never closed.

MEETING IN BIOLOGY CLASS

As a college student, Luke Mitchell sat front and center in Biology 101, highlighters ready, absorbing the professor's words like they were gospel. He was there to ace the class—like he always did—so he could keep stacking credentials like building blocks on his way to med school. Kate sat directly behind him, close enough to hear his muttered commentary when something in the lecture made him roll his eyes.

They were both science-minded. Luke was a classic pre-med student—competitive, skeptical, and always assuming he was the smartest guy in the room. Kate majored in genetics, which Luke figured was a side route to something less intense than what he was doing.

Sometimes they talked after lectures, swapping notes and exchanging light banter. The day after their first major exam, they ran into each other in the hallway outside the lecture hall. Naturally, they started comparing their answers to the questions on the exam. At first it was friendly and curious—maybe even flirty if you squinted. But as they worked down the list of questions, something became clear: They had answered a lot of questions differently.

Luke, of course, was sure he was right. He had studied hard. He knew how to prepare for tests like this using pattern recognition, fast recall, and textbook precision. Kate, on the other hand, was confident in her choices but didn't feel the need to argue about them. He thought she misunderstood the material. She just shrugged and said, "We'll see."

They did see.

Kate got an A+. Luke got an A- and never recovered from the shock.

He'd just been lapped by the quiet, homeschooled girl. She didn't even mention her grade unless someone asked, but Luke knew what it was. And he started watching her more closely. It drove him a little crazy—in the best way.

Kate had grown up attending a small Baptist church in Texas where missionaries were hometown heroes. She had been immersed in ministry from a young age and exposed to gritty stories of people leaving everything to serve in far-off places.

When Kate was in high school, she joined her father on a medical mission trip to China. The leaders had previously been placed under house arrest for sharing the gospel, but they handled the situation so well that the Chinese government invited them back. They agreed but on one condition: They would bring a team of medical professionals only if they were allowed to speak openly about their faith. Permission was granted.

Kate wasn't trained medically yet. She was just a teenager tagging along, helping wherever she could. That's when she saw the young woman. Barely an adult, the woman came into the clinic in serious pain. It turned out to be gallstones, something that would have taken a minor procedure to treat back home. But in rural China, there was no ultrasound machine, which meant no proper diagnostics.

And that woman ended up dying—from *gallstones*.

Kate never forgot her and returned from that mission trip with a fire in her gut. She had always known she wanted to study medicine, but now she knew she wanted to go back to places like that—places where people were dying from things that should be easily and routinely treated. She wanted to help.

Luke didn't know all of that right away, but he knew there was something about Kate that didn't make sense on paper. She was brilliant but not competitive, kind but not a pushover. He was fascinated and for the first time in his life was not the smartest person in the conversation.

Eventually, Kate invited Luke to a campus-wide worship and Bible study session. At first, it was curiosity that made Luke go, and honestly, he was mostly curious about Kate. She lived with a conviction that made him want to know what fueled her. So he went. He sat beside her and listened to the gospel—*really* listened for the first time.

Luke hadn't grown up in church. For him, God was more of an abstract, cultural idea than a person. But as he continued attending and the sermons rolled on, something began to unsettle him. He didn't buy into it all, but it was getting harder to dismiss.

Week after week he kept attending. Questions began to replace his assumptions, and his internal critiques grew quieter. Something was softening, even if he didn't have a name for it yet. It was a slow erosion in his heart like a wall giving way to water.

Somewhere in those months, faith stopped being "Kate's thing" and became his thing too. He didn't walk up the aisle to profess his faith loudly, but he came to believe—deeply. And that belief would set the tone for everything that came next: becoming a doctor, marrying Kate, and saying yes to wherever God would call them.

THEY HAD TO BE UNDONE

For nearly a decade, Luke and Kate Mitchell intentionally prepared to go overseas. They finished their advanced degrees. Kate received her master's degree in physician assistant studies, and Luke wrapped up medical school to enter his residency training in family medicine obstetrics and global health. They got married and grew their family by three children. A lot of life happened in those ten years of schooling and marriage, but one thing remained constant: Both of them sensed that their medical careers would be used in places where access to care was limited.

So they trained earnestly and thoroughly. They went on vision trips and met with sending organizations. They asked God, "Where can we serve most faithfully with what You've given us?" They traveled often, taking short-term trips to Mexico, South America, and even Southeast Asia looking for a fit for their skills and their family. They prepared actively, holding their plans loosely while gaining experience and perspective wherever they went.

And yet, the "where" remained unanswered until the final elective of Luke's residency when he was invited to Myanmar—a country neither of them had ever considered.

Almost immediately, something settled. The tension they'd lived with for years as they waited for clarity seemed to give in. The place, the people, and the need all came together in an unmistakable way.

Not feeling it necessary—or biblical—to have a seminary degree in order to share the gospel, Luke and Kate searched for ways to prepare for life as missionaries without jumping into more schooling. They decided to spend a year in Phoenix, Arizona, for a mission-training opportunity living among refugees from Muslim-majority countries. It wasn't a curriculum-heavy or leadership-driven training; it was just full-time immersion to develop disciple-making as a lifestyle, not just a ministry. It was life among neighbors who didn't speak English, didn't share faith, and didn't owe them anything. It dismantled everything they knew.

Luke and Kate moved into a small apartment surrounded by families from Iraq, Syria, Afghanistan, and Sudan. Both of them, now with advanced medical training, found themselves asking for help to cook dishes with names they couldn't pronounce and fumbling through greetings in Arabic. Their degrees had no bearing on anything there. They were simply learners. It was a deeply humbling season for their entire family.

"We didn't realize how American we were until we were in a context like that," Kate said later.

Being American, she acknowledged, was a gift in many ways, but it wasn't always the best lens through which to see the world. The Mitchells' time in Phoenix revealed just how much of their thinking had been shaped by culture—their views on time, leadership, privacy, and even what successful ministry should look like.

Slowly, those Americanized assumptions began to peel away. They learned to wait longer for conversations and to sit in silence without rushing to fix or explain things. They learned to ask more questions and offer fewer answers. They began to understand that cross-cultural work isn't about delivering solutions but instead about entering stories already in motion and listening long enough to learn what is really needed.

In many ways, that year stripped them of their American way of thinking. They had to be undone so they could become biblical. They weren't trying to erase who they were, but they had to learn to put their culture in its proper context—beneath Scripture, not above it. They started to adopt what they called a "Bible culture," letting the rhythms of humility and hospitality guide them more than efficiency or comfort.

By the end of that year, they were transformed. They were no longer preparing to *fix* anything. They were ready to join the community in Myanmar.

MINISTRY IN THE MARGINS

The Mitchells arrived in Myanmar ready to serve, though the specifics of what that would look like remained murky. They knew without question that God had led them there, but there was no clinic waiting for them. There was no job posting in their specialties. Instead, they entered the country as English teachers. For two fully trained medical professionals, it was not the kind of deployment they had imagined, but they jumped right in.

Kate was placed in a local kindergarten classroom where she found thirty five-year-olds with no structure eyeing the American woman holding flashcards with an enthusiastic smile. On the first day, they stared at her blankly. On the second day, they started climbing on the furniture. By the third day, it was clear they had no concept of classroom discipline.

Kate tried positive reinforcement, gentle corrections, and herding tactics. But it was pure chaos. Eventually, the school brought in an aide, a stoic eighteen-year-old girl whose job was to stand in the corner and whip out a bamboo stick when necessary. She didn't speak much English, but her presence alone made the room slightly less feral.

It wasn't ideal, but it quickly taught Kate that there were no shortcuts to entering another culture. You could bring all the training and good intentions in the world with you, but until you understood how people thought, lived, shared meals, and disciplined their children, you were still on the outside.

While Kate wrangled kindergarteners, Luke taught older

students. His experience was more structured but no less cross-cultural. They hadn't planned to move their family around the world to teach grammar, but English was their entry point.

Though this nonmedical assignment felt strange at first, they discovered almost immediately that relationships always come before calling. And for the people of Myanmar, many of whom had grown up under military control and with civil unrest, trust was not something you could request. It had to be earned—slowly.

Luke and Kate's language skills were clumsy at first. Burmese was difficult. The tonal shifts and scripts were like nothing they had studied. They practiced with taxi drivers and shopkeepers, and their willingness to learn spoke volumes to the locals.

When they were ready, they started their ministry on the floor mats of friends' homes sitting cross-legged and sipping tea they didn't love at first but always accepted. They asked questions and met parents. They learned about the various ethnic groups—the Bamar majority, the Shan, the Paluang, the Kachin, and the Hindu and Muslim people groups. They began to see how religion, language, and history intersected in every invitation to dinner. Only after forming those relationships did they begin to offer medical care.

Home visits became the bridge between their medical training and their mission. At first, it was simple. Someone had a cold. A neighbor's child had a rash. An older woman complained of dizziness. Kate and Luke brought their bags filled with supplies, and they sat and listened. There were no appointments or forms.

Those visits often began with food. The people always offered them a meal, and they never declined. To refuse a meal was to refuse connection. They learned to accept everything—fish soup at nine in the morning, fermented tea leaves, or curries so heavily spiced that it made their eyes water. Hospitality was a language of its own, and the Mitchells became fluent in it long before they could hold a full conversation in Burmese.

The more they visited, the more the word spread. These were foreigners who didn't just teach English at the school; they actually helped. And they didn't discriminate either. Their visits led them to Muslim homes and Christian ones. They treated monks, imams, pregnant mothers, and ailing grandfathers. They adjusted their posture and language to fit each context. In a Buddhist home, they sat lower than the eldest family member. In a Muslim home, they observed customs of modesty and greeting. In Christian homes, they prayed aloud if invited. Over time, they became known as neighbors, no longer foreigners.

That's when they began to understand that this was a ministry among the margins. They had no platform or pulpit, but they did have the floor of someone's home. They committed to the daily slog of sitting in the heat, fumbling through language barriers, eating rice, and having conversations. As they settled into their new home, laying down the efficiency and comforts of the West in favor of the slow, relationship-based pace of the East, they found that the most profound transformation wasn't happening in their patients.

It was happening in them.

THE LEAST COMMON DENOMINATOR

Luke and Kate had originally been invited to Myanmar as part of a team of ten people. At first, their team felt like family. They had trained and prayed together, and they arrived in Myanmar with a shared sense of calling and a deep well of optimism. A few had been to Myanmar before as single men, but now they were all on the field with their families, green and wide-eyed. It was a group partnership with one mission, and they called each other friends.

But ministry is less like a planned project and more like a pressure cooker. And under the weight of cultural strain, spiritual warfare, and sheer exhaustion, cracks began to show.

It started small with disagreements over schedules and mismatched expectations about authority. But slowly, surface tensions deepened into patterns of control and withdrawal. The Mitchells leaned into the coping mechanisms they knew best: people-pleasing and compliance. They had long been wired to make things work. They were the "glue people" who smoothed over conflict, absorbed tension, and did whatever it took to keep the team intact.

But that very instinct became another obstacle on their own team.

They tried to please everyone and be the sounding board for all their teammates, and in doing so, they lost clarity about their own boundaries. Luke took on more tasks, Kate tried to mediate conversations, and others micromanaged both of them. Neither wanted to rock the boat, but the silence became its own form of damage. Their closest friendships began to fray.

One couple they had once called their best friends no longer made eye contact. Tension, spoken and unspoken, simmered. Projects that should have brought joy began to feel like obligations. And Luke and Kate's home, once a place of rest, became a second office where late-night debriefs about the situation developed into anxiety loops and marital strife.

Kate wanted her husband to protect her more and provide a louder voice against what felt very much like disrespect from her teammates. Luke wanted to believe that silence among the group meant peace, which was enough for him to keep going every day with eyes on the mission, not the mess. During that season, they both had to confront a truth they hadn't wanted to face: The mission field was becoming a threat to their marriage.

So they drew a line. They stepped back from the idea that team unity had to come before everything else. They realized they could not keep sacrificing their own peace for the appearance of cohesion. They called this honor "the least common denominator"—if nothing else was working around them, at the very least their marriage had to work. The relationship in their home had to be healed before they could even consider healing relationships outside of it.

So they started protecting their evenings, turning off their phones, and saying no to things that drained their energy. They stopped letting ministry spill into every conversation every hour. Slowly they began to rebuild their relationship with each other and with God who had called them into this ministry in the first place.

And then, just as they began to find footing as a couple again, the world shut down.

COVID-19 swept through Myanmar, closing borders and gobbling up medical supplies. In the local religious culture, self-sacrifice held no value. Why would educated professionals foolishly risk their lives? Suddenly, every health clinic and hospital closed.

Many expats left Myanmar thinking they had to seek out a temporary refuge, but they ended up getting stuck. Some never returned. Luke and Kate decided to stay.

They didn't know what else to do, and people needed care. They had the training and the calling. So they asked for courage and a supernatural trust in God. Perhaps that is what they had been called to do all along, they reasoned. They pressed on, raising their children to become their new teammates on the field.

They opened a clinic, the only remaining point of care in the region. They scrambled to get the first wave of vaccines, coordinating with expat networks and praying that the shipments would arrive in time.

As their medical clinic became a fixture in the community, government officials approached them with a request to offer obstetric care and deliver babies. With Luke's medical training, they knew this was what they were made for. Over the next three years, they delivered more than 300 children. Kate trained local women to support laboring mothers, and Luke managed triage under conditions he never would have imagined in residency—no power and a staff made up of local laypeople they had trained over the past several years of home visits. Strangely, it worked.

Stripped of the formality of titles, schedules, and even team meetings, they found something purer. Their kids helped translate conversations and pass supplies. Neighbors turned into nurses. The lines outside the clinic grew long.

Relational survival, they learned, didn't come from rigid roles or idealistic hierarchy. It came from humility, knowing when to release control, and focusing on the least common denominator. In those long months of masks and birth cries, the Mitchell family didn't just serve the community. They became one.

A FAMILY OF REFUGEES

Seven years into life as overseas missionaries, Luke and Kate were no longer green and wide-eyed. They had established roots that the pandemic only strengthened. Their Burmese had improved. Their children were accustomed to life in a developing country— more comfortable with rice than potatoes. And their family had grown. In addition to their four biological children, they had adopted their eldest, Hannah, from Myanmar. She had become both a daughter and a symbol of their love for the country.

Myanmar was their home … until the coup happened.

In early 2023, rising tensions in the country erupted into chaos. The military's power grab spread fear while government structures collapsed, checkpoints multiplied, and whispers of people being "disappeared" reached their own neighborhood. The air, always heavy with humidity, now also carried a tension that no amount of prayer could deflect.

When it became obvious that there was no other choice, Luke and Kate said the briefest of goodbyes, locked up the clinic, and found someone to lead them out of the country. Worst of all, in the chaos of evacuation, Hannah was unable to travel with them. The logistics and legal barriers were insurmountable at that time. So they left her behind, carrying the weight of separation and not knowing how, when, or if they'd be reunited.

The rest of the family landed in what was technically their hometown in Texas, but they found it emotionally unrecognizable. After living in a war zone, everything felt excessive. Supermarkets were the first shock. The shelves were overflowing, and the cereal aisle alone stretched longer than the entire hallway in their clinic. The abundance was overwhelming for the Mitchell children who had spent most if not all of their childhood in the stark contrast of minimalism.

In Myanmar, hospitality looked like walking through doors without knocking, sharing meals in plastic bowls, or sitting for hours with neighbors who had nothing but still gave freely. In Texas, people rushed through conversations and checked their phones mid-sentence. Small talk felt insufferable. Kate found herself smiling politely through gatherings and then crying in the car on the way home. Luke didn't even have language for what he felt—only a heaviness in his chest.

They were safe, but they were not settled.

The United States had once been their comfort zone, but now

it felt disorienting like walking through a former life wearing someone else's shoes. They missed the community rhythms of Myanmar, the spontaneous visits, the interdependence, and the absence of social media. They missed the people and the shared sense of spiritual hunger.

More than anything, they missed Hannah.

Displacement had redefined them. Their identity had once been so clear—doctors, missionaries, parents. Now it was layered with confusion and waiting.

They were wanderers, pilgrims, refugees.

STILL NOT HOME

For Luke and Kate, the weight of that closed door was indescribably heavy. They missed the clinic and their neighbors. They missed the feeling of belonging to a community. Most of their time was spent counseling, encouraging supporters, and speaking about their experiences. Around March 2024, a longtime friend invited Luke to work at a hospital and medical school in Thailand in order to share the gospel with students and faculty, patients in the community, and thousands of displaced Myanmar ethnic peoples who were living there.

This caught Luke's attention. Something in it felt open—not quite like going back to Myanmar but at least *toward* Myanmar. He and Kate decided to jump at the opportunity to move back around the globe. They didn't have the confidence that it was a long-term mission field, but they had a convicted willingness to try. They chose a city in northern Thailand about thirty minutes from the Myanmar border—close enough to give them hope, to let them feel connected to their home, and to pursue reunification with Hannah.

No words can capture the ache of separation between a parent and a child or the relief of reunion. Hannah crossed the border safely and entered their new home with the same quiet courage that had marked her life from the beginning. The family was whole again.

But their world wasn't.

Thailand, though peaceful and safe, wasn't home—not for them and not for the thousands of Myanmar refugees crossing into camps nearby. The language was new again, and the culture was more reserved. The Thai people were kind but distant, especially to the flood of refugees arriving daily. Refugees were not seen as guests but as voiceless burdens. They were not welcome and did not receive any state-funded aid.

For the Mitchells, it was like living with a mirror held up. Their own sense of displacement was reflected in the face of every refugee at the camp. A new ministry was born there in the tents and border clinics that popped up, among undergraduate and medical students, among refugees and day laborers, and among people on the fringes of society. As Luke and Kate worked, they welcomed old teammates and former clinic aides who had also fled Myanmar.

Everything started over. Luke resumed teaching to train more medical aides. Kate helped coordinate mobile care to travel to new camps with medical supplies.

The work has since grown to include much more than medicine. The Mitchells go to a few mobile clinics and help at the refugee camps when they can, and the Lord has pulled out some of their other giftings as well such as leading women (Myanmar, expat, and Thai) in worship through art and helping empower other Myanmar believers doing ministry in Thailand. They host retreats for those in need of soul healing.

The work in Thailand is necessary, but it still isn't home.

As of this writing, much of Myanmar remains locked down, politically fractured, and unsafe for return. The village where the Mitchells lived and the surrounding regions remain closed and under control of ethnic and political factions. Every refugee they meet longs to go back. Even now as fellow exiles, Luke and Kate pray regularly for the day they'll return to Myanmar to reopen their clinic, walk the streets they once called home, and embrace neighbors and friends they didn't get to say goodbye to.

Their calling hasn't changed, but their understanding of it has. Geography doesn't need to align with their vision. Though their hearts ache for home, the map is less important than the people in front of them. In the shared humanity of living as refugees, they get to see Christ work.

They might still be wandering, but they are not lost.

MY TAKE: FAITH IN THE IN-BETWEEN

Luke and Kate began their years of missionary service by living with refugees, and now in a way, they have become refugees themselves. They left their home country, answered God's call, and built a life in a foreign land—only to see it dismantled by forces entirely out of their control. Now displaced in Thailand, they carry both the burden and the perspective of those they originally went to serve. That's a deeply humbling experience.

And that refugee identity isn't just theirs; it also extends to their children. As third-culture children, they are being raised between worlds. The United States doesn't feel like home, and neither does Thailand. Myanmar was the only home they'd ever really known, and the sudden evacuation was extremely disorienting for them. Like many missionary kids, they carry a sense of being wanderers, never fully landing. This is a hidden cost of missions we don't talk about enough. Answering God's call can uproot the entire family, sometimes permanently.

This is part of the risk of obedience. When you step into God's calling, there's no guarantee of stability or permanence. Sometimes you think you'll only be there a short while, and end up staying much longer. Sometimes you go expecting to stay for life, but God moves you unexpectedly. Either way, you end up living with the consequences of that surrender, especially as a parent trying to discern what that means for your kids.

But here's what gives me hope: Even in displacement, God isn't done writing the story. The Mitchells' hearts are still tethered to Myanmar, and who knows what doors God might open in the future. In the meantime, as a family they serve, they wait, and they trust.

CHAPTER 5

DO WHAT YOU'RE CALLED TO DO

DAVID AND JOY BOSTON

They hadn't even been married a week when David Boston found himself sweating in the middle of rural Mozambique. He held a plastic bucket under a broken shower pipe and wondered how exactly this counted as a honeymoon.

Before they said their vows, David and his new wife, Joy, had committed to a short-term medical mission trip. He didn't realize that meant staying in a beat-up house with no air conditioning, limited electricity, and a toilet that only flushed if someone

Do What You're Called to Do | **59**

remembered to pour enough water into the tank. The romance was unconventional to say the least.

Despite all that, something about it felt right—messy and exhausting but right. Due to David's work schedule, Joy had arrived a couple days ahead of him, and by the time he stepped off the plane, she had the whole operation running like a well-oiled machine. She was clearly in her element, unshaken by the chaos around her.

Back in the States, David worked as an emergency room doctor. He made quick, life-saving decisions and handled medical emergencies with wisdom and good instincts. Here, in the chaotic rural jungle, he wasn't quite sure where he fit. So he just watched and paid attention.

In the stillness, he noticed something that hadn't hit him before: No one was really talking to the local staff. They were working hard, but the relationships—the real human connections—felt thin. That realization unsettled him.

The whole purpose of being there was to serve, yes. But it was also to know people, to learn their stories, and to walk with them, not just work *around* them. He began to see that the missing piece wasn't the need for more doctors or more efficiency. He realized the big need was for genuine human connection.

That's when David met Dondo, the Mozambican medical director who wasn't impressed with the parade of white missionary do-gooders showing up with big plans to fix everything and save everyone.

David sensed it immediately—the careful glances, the polite distance. Dondo had seen people like David and Joy before—Westerners who showed up with energy and resources, who stayed for a moment, made decisions, and moved on. David didn't blame Dondo for the skepticism. Still, he wanted to bridge the gap. So he asked Dondo to dinner. Dondo agreed but showed no enthusiasm.

Together, they found a dim shack with rickety tables and

a crooked menu nailed to the wall. It only listed two things: chicken or beef.

David, hoping to keep things simple, said "chicken."

The server nodded, disappeared, and then returned a few minutes later to say, "No chicken. Only beef."

David shrugged and switched to beef.

A moment later, the server came back. "We have chicken now."

David glanced at Dondo who gave a rare, amused smile.

They sat in silence for a few minutes, and then without a word, a man pedaled up on a bicycle with two live chickens dangling from the handlebars. The server walked out, grabbed one, and disappeared behind a curtain. Somewhere in the back, a cleaver hit wood. It wasn't exactly fine dining, but the tension between the two doctors was officially cut as they shared their first laugh.

After that, conversation came slowly, built out of gestures, broken English, and halted Portuguese. Dondo spoke carefully. David listened hard.

When the silence stretched too long, David reached into his bag and pulled out his CD player. He cracked it open without thinking, and Dondo caught a glimpse of the disc inside.

Bruce Springsteen.

Dondo's eyes lit up. He pointed. "Bruce!" he said, grinning. It was just one word, but it felt like a bridge. They pressed *play* on small headphones and ramped up the volume so they could both hear the song. As they bopped their heads to the beat, something softened between them.

In that small, smoky shack, David's mission became clear. The medical work that he and Joy had come to do mattered. Of course it did. But healing diseases and treating injuries at the local hospital wasn't their only calling.

Dondo didn't need another solution from the West. He needed someone who saw him, who cared enough to share a meal and stay long enough to build trust. So with chicken on the grill and Springsteen in his ears, David began to understand what being on a mission really meant.

OPPOSITES ATTRACT

David didn't grow up hearing Bible stories at bedtime, and his family didn't gather around the dinner table for prayer. They didn't exactly shun faith; it just didn't show up. Holidays came and went without much mention. Church was simply a building other people visited, and God was an idea reserved for weddings and funerals. David wasn't hostile to belief; he just didn't need it.

By the time David was a teenager, he had decided that religion wasn't for him. He trusted what he could measure and see. He developed a love for science and a dream of practicing medicine. The life of a doctor felt solid, real, and testable. It gave him answers. And for a while, that was enough.

He moved through school with a steady hand and a sharp mind, never one to be rattled. That helped in his medical training, and soon he found his rhythm in the intensity of hospital life. The chaos of the ER made sense to him in a way that faith never had. He assessed, he acted, and he moved on.

Joy's world looked nothing like that. She had grown up in a Southern Baptist church where Sunday mornings meant dresses, pews, and choir music that floated to the rafters. She could recite Bible verses before she understood half of what they meant.

Missions were talked about often—men and women on the far side of the globe giving their lives away for the sake of the gospel. She listened to their stories wide-eyed and curious on church nights. She never quite imagined herself in their shoes, but she always felt a little tug.

In Joy's childhood home, God was a presence—someone she turned to when things were good and when they weren't. As she grew older, that quiet tug toward service started to pull a little harder. In high school, she began thinking about medicine, not because she wanted prestige or a big paycheck but because she felt drawn to people in need. Healing felt like something holy.

By the time Joy reached medical school, she already carried a sense of calling. It wasn't loud. She wasn't the type to stand on a stage or speak in big, sweeping declarations. But it was there—a quiet belief that her work, if offered to God, could matter beyond the clinic walls. She didn't have all the answers, but she had a steady kind of certainty.

David hadn't ever met anyone like her. They crossed paths in residency. Joy had just finished a brutal stretch in the neonatal intensive care unit (NICU), and David was her upper-level resident as she rotated into internal medicine. He knew she was post-call and half-delirious with exhaustion. So he did something small. He made a round on all her patients before she arrived and told her to go home and rest.

It wasn't a grand gesture, but it left an impression, and Joy noticed the kindness. The next day, she showed up to work a little more awake and a little more curious.

They started slowly with a few late-night shifts and some shared jokes in the hallway. David brought Joy cheesecake when she was on call, which she pretended not to read too much into. She laughed at his dry humor, and he admired her focus. There was an ease between them—unspoken, unforced.

Before long, they weren't just sharing shifts; they were sharing long talks and future plans. What started as quiet chemistry between opposites had grown into an undeniable attraction. By the time residency ended, there wasn't a question of *if*—just *when*.

They were in it for the long haul.

THE LATE BLOOMER

At the time, Joy already knew who she was and what she believed spiritually. David didn't. But he didn't shy away from it either. He asked questions and listened carefully. To David, faith had always seemed like a foreign language, and not an especially useful one at that.

But Joy's quiet conviction stirred something in him. She didn't try to preach or persuade. She just lived her faith like she lived everything else, with integrity, steadiness, and no need to draw attention to it.

In the early days of their relationship, David started spending time with a local pastor. The pastor wasn't out to win an argument. He simply met David where he was—over coffee, in conversation. They talked about faith, sure, but they also talked about life, disappointment, and questions that didn't have easy answers. The pastor never pushed. He just stayed and asked good questions. He offered David space to think out loud.

He showed David how to build a long-term, genuine relationship with another human being, and over time something in David's heart began to shift. Things he had once dismissed started to feel weightier. His skepticism softened. He never stopped asking hard questions, but now his curiosity began to come from a different place. It was no longer disbelief but a yearning to learn more. Life started to feel richer and fuller.

It wasn't sudden. There was no lightning bolt or dramatic altar call, just consistent respect and engagement. This pastor had a way of making faith feel like an invitation.

One day, after months of walking that path together, David realized he was ready. He didn't have it all figured out, but he believed enough to step forward and cross the line of faith. He called the pastor, and they talked and prayed about David's decision.

At the age of thirty, David was baptized. A "late bloomer Christian" he called himself later. But to him, it didn't feel late. It felt right, like he'd finally stopped resisting something that had been there all along.

Joy didn't react with fanfare. She didn't try to take credit. She just stood beside him that day, grateful, steady, and full of quiet joy. Their stories had started from two different worlds with two different understandings of faith. But somehow their lives were beginning to unfold side by side.

"I'LL NEVER MOVE OVERSEAS"

David never imagined doing mission work full-time. He enjoyed the short-term trips that Joy introduced him to—a few weeks here, a month there, enough to do some good, offer what he could, and then come home. After their wedding, Mozambique sparked something in him, especially that dinner with Dondo. He loved the work, but he also loved coming back to the rhythm of home, the structure, and the financial security. He said half-seriously and half-defensively, "I'll never move overseas."

But in those early years of marriage, he and Joy kept circling the conversation about a long-term mission assignment.

What would it look like to go? To really *go?*

Joy would have packed up and left the next day. Missions had been a thread running through her story since she was young, woven into Sunday school lessons, church slideshows, and campfire testimonies. She wasn't naive about how hard it would be, but she felt the pull, and it never quite let go.

David was interested but also practical. He wouldn't go without a financial safety net. If God gave them one, then maybe he'd consider it.

Without a unified answer, life went on. They based their medical practices in Louisville, and their family grew. The idea of moving overseas with young children, one of them on the autism spectrum, felt less like an adventure and more like a logistical impossibility. David worked full-time in emergency medicine. Joy had a job she loved at a community clinic.

Life was full, busy, and good. But the calling to go overseas persisted.

After a while, they started to wonder if maybe their hesitation wasn't caution or wisdom but rather fear and disbelief in God's provision. *Were they being unfaithful?* Joy argued that maybe the calling would never fade because it was waiting to be answered.

In response, David pointed out that the numbers in their budget didn't lie. They had a mountain of medical school debt, a mortgage, groceries to buy for a family of five, and college savings to build for three kids. He knew they couldn't pay their debts with good intentions—even missionary ones.

He just couldn't stomach the idea of dragging his family into a life where money was always tight and where every decision hinged on someone else's donation. That's what scared him more than anything—not the move, not the culture shock, but the financial uncertainty and the responsibility to provide for his family in a poverty-stricken country.

Knowing that they needed unity in their marriage, David and Joy explored options for financial support. They prayed and waited for God's provision. That's when they found MedSend, a Christian nonprofit that offered to pay off educational loans for medical professionals serving abroad.

David couldn't believe it at first. It felt too simple, too generous, like there would be a catch. But it was real. MedSend didn't just lift a financial burden; it opened a door that David had stood adamantly in front of with crossed arms.

Now with a huge part of the financial obstacle taken care of, David was able to consider long-term missions with a softer heart. He knew that if money didn't hold him back, he was willing to go. MedSend was the sign he had been waiting for. It was time to water the seed of evangelical conviction God had planted in Mozambique.

With newfound confidence in their unity, David and Joy made a long-term plan to serve in Cambodia. The road there wasn't perfect. It wasn't predictable. But it was possible because of God.

WHATEVER BUGS YOU HERE WILL ELEPHANT YOU THERE

Culture shock didn't hit all at once. Cambodia met them with humidity, unfamiliar rhythms, and a thousand small adjustments that added up fast. Nothing came easily—not groceries, not electricity, not plumbing. Everything they'd known as "normal" back home disappeared in the rearview mirror, replaced by a new life that constantly asked more of them.

Buying milk, wiring money, making a fan work—each required a kind of perseverance they didn't always have and a cultural flexibility they were still learning to build. The heat was constant. The traffic was chaotic. The language was unfamiliar and difficult to grasp. There were days it felt like everything took twice the energy and gave back half the result.

"Whatever bugs you here will elephant you there," a friend told Joy before they left. Now that they were abroad, it became a family motto of sorts—an honest acknowledgment that the little irritations would grow into massive burdens if they left them unchecked.

A clogged drain in Kentucky? Annoying.

A clogged drain in Cambodia with no hardware store, no plumber, and no clean water? That could bring a man to his knees.

Fatigue lowered patience. Miscommunication was frequent. And the pressure to keep serving often left little room to process what was happening between them.

In that pressure cooker, David and Joy had to learn a new way to respond to each other. That's when the phrase *God knows* started showing up between them.

Often at the end of a long day or a hard conversation, the phrase became their secret message to spur one another on. It was a shared breath, a mutual surrender when neither had the answer but both still needed grace.

God knows became their shorthand for empathy.

They also learned the value of small, intentional practices. Scheduling time together wasn't romantic; it was survival. Even if it was just sitting in silence over coffee while the kids watched a movie, they fought for moments that reminded them they were still on the same team. Unity didn't happen by accident. It wasn't a natural byproduct of a shared calling.

It came by choice, again and again, through choosing forgiveness, choosing to laugh when they wanted to yell, or saying "I'm sorry" even when they weren't entirely sure they were wrong. It was whispering *God knows* when they weren't sure if they could stand another day in Cambodia.

In choosing unity, David and Joy realized that the reason they could stay was because of God's quiet and steady presence in the middle of their mess.

SOMEONE'S CAREER HAD TO
GO DOWN THE TOILET

David and Joy arrived in Cambodia with three kids under the age of six. Two of them were adopted. Their oldest was autistic. He was high-functioning and bright, but change overwhelmed him to the point of tantrums. The idea of pulling up roots and starting over in Southeast Asia was asking the impossible of him. As parents, David and Joy fully expected a season of meltdowns as they began their life abroad.

But to everyone's surprise—especially David's—their son adjusted. And he didn't just tolerate the new lifestyle. Somehow he was the one in the family who thrived. Something about the pace, the predictability of village life, and the kindness of the Cambodian people seemed to calm him. The culture didn't stigmatize his differences. If anything, it absorbed them with quiet grace. What David feared might break their son somehow made him feel at home.

But Joy paid a different price in their new home. She had trained for years to be a pediatrician with long nights, long rotations, and long seasons of giving everything she had to medicine. Healing children, supporting families, and advocating for the vulnerable were who she was. By the time she and David moved to Cambodia, she had built a career that felt meaningful.

And then it all had to be put on hold. They had three children, each with unique needs, and the options for education overseas were lacking.

Someone had to homeschool them.

Someone had to figure out groceries and routines in a new home.

Someone had to consider safety and survival in a developing country.

And that someone was Joy.

"Someone's career had to go down the toilet, and it was mine," she said with a dry smile that only half-disguised the weight of the truth.

It wasn't bitterness—just honesty. Her days, once spent diagnosing patients and solving medical problems, now revolved around phonics lessons, sensory meltdowns, and figuring out how to make dinner with whatever ingredients the market had that day. Behavior charts replaced patient charts. Her stethoscope gathered dust in a drawer. And while she wouldn't have chosen this path on her own, it chose her.

Joy never saw herself as a martyr. In the mess and the monotony, something deeper began to take root. She started to realize that this hard, hidden work of loving and shaping her children wasn't a detour from her purpose; it was her purpose. Holding her child through a meltdown and teaching each of her kids to read were moments that didn't make headlines but built something important.

And Joy didn't give her career up entirely. One day a week, she still practiced medicine by working at an abuse recovery clinic. It wasn't glamorous, and it certainly wasn't easy, but it kept part of her professional heart alive. That one day anchored her and reminded her of the skills she still carried and the lives she still had the power to touch. In the domestic moments that felt consumed by her children's needs, the clinic gave her a space to remember her own voice.

It wasn't balance exactly. It was more like obedience—saying yes to the life in front of her. It didn't look like what she imagined back in medical school because she had given up the clean and clear career path for something messier, something harder. But looking back, she wouldn't change a thing.

STRANGELY PATIENT

Being Christians in a predominantly Buddhist country came with its own quiet tension. Because David and Joy's medical expertise became a presence at four hospitals in the region, the government knew who they were and largely respected them. But spiritual openness didn't come easily.

In many communities, converting to Christianity meant losing family ties, business connections, and sometimes an entire social circle. The people they served weren't hostile, but they were cautious. "Yes, yes," was the default answer—polite agreement without real conviction. David and Joy quickly realized that spiritual progress couldn't be measured by quick conversions or checkboxes. It had to grow organically and often invisibly.

David believed deeply that the only way forward was long-term relationship-building. He trusted that showing up, staying present, and living with integrity might say more about Jesus than any sermon ever could.

David was strangely patient when it came to spiritual transformation. He traced it all the way back to his own pastor's gentle influence before he converted to the faith. Patience had also worked well in Mozambique. During the shared meal with Dondo, a simple CD cracked a wall that words couldn't touch. David had learned something. Real relationships take time, and he wasn't in a rush.

Joy respected that, but it tugged at something inside her. She had grown up in a world where evangelism was urgent. As a Southern Baptist, she never knew if someone would get another chance to hear the gospel. She was taught not to wait. She was supposed to act. Salvation was a now-or-never kind of decision.

So when weeks turned into months and they still hadn't had any "spiritual conversations" with people, Joy wrestled with the tension.

Were they speaking boldly enough?
Were they reaching far enough?
Were they being too passive?

Joy never doubted David's faith, but sometimes she wondered if he understood the stakes.

They talked about it often—sometimes gently, sometimes with frustration simmering. David explained that evangelism without relationships felt hollow to him. Joy responded that silence could be just as damaging, especially in a place where people barely knew the gospel.

Their different upbringings weren't just backgrounds; they were lenses. David, newer to faith and still amazed by grace, didn't want to tread too hard on shaky ground. Joy, raised in the faith, felt the weight of responsibility like a ticking clock.

Both of them knew their hearts for sharing Jesus were aligned. But their methods came from different life stories and different spiritual DNA.

In the middle of all of it, they had one constant lifeline: their mentor, Rich. He didn't offer easy answers or tidy theology. What he offered was a consistent and compassionate relationship.

When Joy questioned whether they were making any difference at all, Rich asked questions and listened. Slowly he reminded them who they were, whose they were, and what they were—and weren't—called to do. That reminder was freeing. They didn't need to force fruit. They just needed to be present, patient, and honest. Even if the work was slower than they'd expected, the results would make a real difference.

Rich had a way of helping them zoom out—past the moment, past the pressure—and remember the bigger picture. They were called. They were equipped. They were not failing just because it felt hard.

The tension didn't resolve cleanly. There was no single moment when they suddenly landed on the same page. But over time, they began to see that both of their evangelical instincts held wisdom.

Joy started to understand that David's slowness wasn't hesitation; it was reverence. It came from a place of deep respect for the people they served and the weight of their cultural context. And David began to see that Joy's urgency wasn't pressure; it was love. It came from a lifetime of believing that the best gift you could give someone was the gospel truth spoken plainly.

Somewhere between their styles, the mission began to take shape. Together they learned to trust the long game—to plant seeds without knowing if they'd ever see them bloom, to believe that God could do more with their small, steady faithfulness than with any grand plan they might try to force. And that was enough.

DO WHAT YOU ARE CALLED TO DO

We didn't create Cambodia.

In that simple sentence lives a world of freedom. It is an acknowledgment that David and Joy were never meant to carry the full weight of transformation. That was never the assignment.

They came to serve, love, and offer what they had. But they couldn't fix a country. They couldn't rewrite culture. And they weren't the heroes of anyone's story.

Early on they felt the pressure to do more, save more, reach farther, and bear fruit that could be measured, photographed, and sent back home in newsletters. But over time, they began to see the danger in those expectations. That kind of pressure didn't just strain their marriage; it risked distorting their relationships with the people they'd come to serve.

When they decided to do just what they were called to do, they became lighter, truer, and more available. Humility didn't shrink their purpose; it clarified it. They learned to ask better questions, notice the nuances more, and build relationships that weren't dependent on outcomes. Somehow that made space for real connection, the kind that lasts longer than any project or program.

Rather than asking, *How much can we fix?* they began to ask, *What is our part to do?*

That part was not everything, just the part entrusted to them—to be present, to be faithful, and to be human, honest, and willing. In the end, that is more than enough.

MY TAKE: WHEN FAITH FINDS YOU

God often surprises us, especially when we tell Him what we're *not* going to do. "I'll never become a Christian." "I'll never be a missionary." Those kinds of declarations seem to be God's favorite starting points.

David was adamant, and yet God brought a missionary-hearted woman into his life and patiently and persistently led him toward the exact calling he had resisted. Joy's quiet but unwavering faith and a faithful pastor who walked beside David were signs of God's gentle persistence and the way He uses others to draw us to Himself.

I resonate with that deeply. I was thirty-two when I was baptized—darn near ancient—and my own journey to faith included a wife who lived it before I believed it and a pastor who patiently showed me the difference between religion and relationship, between a harsh, distant God and a loving Father who actually wanted to know me.

If you're a pastor or mentor wondering if your investment is making a difference, let this encourage you: It might take time, but seeds planted in faith often bear fruit later. And if you're someone who feels like you're late to the game, don't count yourself out. God has a long history of using late bloomers.

I also want to pause and acknowledge what David and Joy Boston are up against. Their willingness to bring hope and healing in a context like Cambodia where Buddhist and animist worldviews often resist Christian compassion is no small thing. In those cultures, suffering is seen as deserved, the result of past lives. You're not expected to help the suffering; you're expected to step aside and let them pay their debt.

But then missionaries like David and Joy show up carrying a radically different message. Every person is made in the image of God and has inherent value. Love is the driving force behind their service. And eventually, someone asks, "Why are you here?"

That's the open door. That's the moment when they get to say, "Because I serve a God who loves you, and He sent me to care for you." In that answer, seeds are planted, and truth begins to take root.

That's the power of healthcare missions. It earns you the right to speak because you've paid the price in service, compassion, and staying when others might walk away.

CHAPTER 6

EVEN IN LOSS, HE IS STILL GOOD

S E T H   A N D   R E B E C C A   M A L L A Y

R ebecca Mallay stood just outside the hospital room, her hands shaking. Her daughter Elora, just six weeks old, struggled to breathe. The nurses and doctors moved fast, and now they crowded around her tiny daughter. They spoke in clipped, urgent tones, adjusting wires, and calling for things Rebecca didn't understand. No one looked her in the eye. No one had time to explain.

Rebecca had never felt so helpless.

Her legs carried her to the bathroom down the hall where she shut the door and finally let herself fall apart. Tears came fast and silent. Words tumbled out of her mouth in some sort of prayer—raw and honest.

Rebecca was scared and desperate. She sat there crying for several minutes that stretched into the night. No one even looked for her, which made her more panicked about the gravity of the situation. She cried until her breathing steadied.

Then somehow in the middle of her slow sobbing, a quiet thought rose up from deep inside: *She's not mine. She's Yours.*

It wasn't resignation or defeat. Instead, it was surrender.

"I can't control this," she whispered. "You gave her to me, Lord. You love her more than I ever could. If it's time for her to go, I trust You. But *please*, if I can, I want to keep her."

That prayer—broken, honest, and full of trembling hope—marked something in Rebecca. Elora would eventually recover and grow up strong and healthy. But something shifted in Rebecca that night in the hospital bathroom. She released her child into the hands of a faithful God and felt His peace meet her in the release.

She didn't know it then, but this was God's heart preparation—the first invitation into the practice of lament, loosening her grip, trusting God with the most precious things, and learning to worship even while her heart broke.

ALIGNED CALLINGS, ALIGNED HEARTS

Seth Mallay knew grief long before he could name it. When he was just four years old, his baby brother died of a brain tumor. Not long after, his uncle took his own life. Those events didn't make much sense to a child, but they left a mark. Death wasn't just something that happened to other people. It was something that could show up in your own home, take someone you loved, and leave the air heavy with silence.

For most kids, childhood is light and carefree. Seth had plenty of those moments, too, but his view of the world was shaped by the reality that sorrow could find you, even in a loving home and even when you prayed.

While other kids his age were thinking about bikes or cartoons, Seth found himself asking deeper questions. He didn't have fancy words for them, but the thoughts were there: *Why do people hurt? Where do they go when they die? What can I do to help?*

By the time he was seven, Seth was sitting in a Sunday school class when the teacher asked the kids to think about what they wanted to be when they grew up. He didn't even hesitate: "I think God wants me to be a missionary doctor."

He didn't know exactly what that meant. No one in his immediate family had gone into medicine. They weren't well-connected. They didn't have money for expensive schools. But he felt a quiet certainty that God had something for him to do, and it would involve bringing help and hope to people who were suffering.

Rebecca's world looked a little different.

She was born in Brazil, the daughter of church-planting missionaries who had grown up as missionary kids. Missions was more than a career path in her family; it was a way of life, woven into her family's DNA. She was surrounded by stories of faith, sacrifice, and people coming to know Jesus in remote places.

As a little girl, she listened wide-eyed to the stories her parents told around the dinner table and imagined herself doing the same thing someday. But what tugged at her heart most was the idea of medical missions. She wasn't drawn to become a doctor, but the thought of walking alongside someone in medicine—of being a support, a partner in that kind of work—stuck with her.

She began praying for it, even as a child. "Lord, if that's what you want, bring someone into my life who's called to medical missions." It felt oddly specific, but the desire was steady.

Years passed. Rebecca's family eventually moved back to the United States so she could begin college. Meanwhile, Seth was also making his way through school, still holding on to that calling from childhood. They met at a birthday party, introduced by mutual friends in Michigan.

It wasn't anything flashy or romantic, just two young adults talking about life. But when Seth casually mentioned that he wanted to become a medical missionary, Rebecca's heart jumped.

She hadn't expected that. The words felt like an echo of the prayers she'd prayed as a girl. She didn't say anything right away, but she listened closely. The more he shared, the more she recognized something familiar—not just in the calling but in the spirit behind it.

That first conversation turned into more conversations. They shared stories about their childhoods, their faith, and their dreams. They asked each other big questions and gave honest answers. There was a sense of ease, mutual respect, and curiosity.

What started as friendship deepened with time because they genuinely *liked* each other. They made each other laugh and talked easily, and most importantly, their hearts were pointed in the same direction.

It didn't take long for both of them to recognize that their relationship was the beginning of something neither of them actively looked for but both had quietly hoped for all along.

HEART PREPARATION

Seth and Rebecca married young; she was twenty-one, and he was just twenty. Within a year, they started having kids, eventually growing their family by six children. They didn't have much, but they had each other, a shared calling, and just enough faith to take the next step. Seth wasn't even in medical school yet when they said "I do." But they knew they were headed for medical missions. That much had always been clear.

Their early married life was quiet, but things didn't come easily. They had financial stress that young people in school and without jobs naturally have. A lot of the time, that financial stress bled into emotional stress. They lived in a small house in a small town in Michigan with limited job opportunities. They were near their families, but Rebecca struggled to find work.

Money was tight—so tight they could only afford to apply to one medical school. It was a risk, but they had no choice. They drained their savings, took out loans, and even borrowed cash the old-fashioned way just to cover the one application and interview costs. The plan wasn't airtight, but they were relying on God to keep opening the right doors at the right time.

And God did. Seth was accepted into Michigan State University's College of Osteopathic Medicine, and the slow march toward medical missions officially began.

During those years, Rebecca stepped fully into her role as the supporter spouse. She handled the paperwork, managed their home, and raised their children—all while Seth poured himself into studying. There was no room for anything but obedience and trust that they were following the Lord's plan for their lives.

One of the hardest moments came after they moved to Traverse City, Michigan, a beautiful lakeside town where Seth was finishing a portion of his medical training. Rebecca loved it there. She had friends, and the family could walk to the park and the beach. For a brief season, life felt easy—charming even. So when Seth applied for residency, they both hoped it would be there. Rebecca quietly longed for it.

But Seth wasn't matched to Traverse City. Instead, he was placed in a small town near the Indiana state line with no beaches and no vibrant community, just farmland and quiet roads. Rebecca was crushed. It felt like a loss. But something unexpected happened in that season. They found a church in that little town—nothing flashy but full of people who believed in missions, people who reminded them why they had started this journey in the first place.

Looking back, Rebecca sees it clearly. If they had stayed in Traverse City with its comfort and charm, it might have been harder to leave. Her heart might have clung too tightly. God was consistently teaching her to hold everything in her life loosely—to release not just the big dreams but the little comforts too. Seth felt it too.

They didn't know it then, but those small acts of letting go were laying the groundwork for the hardest surrender of all. One day they would be asked to release the most precious thing in their lives. But even then—even through tears—they would recognize the pattern. They had been practicing this all along—trusting a faithful God who never wastes a sacrifice and never calls without providing His presence in return.

They were learning that letting go wasn't about loss. It was about making space for grace. And in every surrender, God was preparing them for the kind of life that walks through sorrow with open hands and eyes fixed on heaven.

LEANING INTO LAMENT

After Seth completed medical school and residency, he and Rebecca knew it was time to take the next step toward medical missions. At a medical missions conference in Louisville, Kentucky, they met representatives from an organization that was looking for physicians who were called to serve overseas. Seth and Rebecca immediately sensed this was the open door they had been praying for and confidently stepped through it.

Years of preparation, schooling, and surrender led them to their first mission assignment in Togo, West Africa. When Seth and Rebecca first stepped onto that red soil, it felt like a dream finally realized.

However, it didn't take long for the weight of the work to settle onto their shoulders. Medical missions in Togo wasn't just challenging; it was heartbreaking. Patients arrived too late, resources were limited, and suffering was constant. Every week brought new stories of loss. Children died from malaria. Mothers bled out during childbirth. Simple infections turned fatal.

Seth struggled most with the sheer volume of death. He had been trained to help and heal, but too often it felt like all he could do was watch people slip away. The questions pressed in on him daily: *If God is good, why is this happening? Is He not good? Is He not all powerful?*

The answers didn't come in quick, comforting phrases. But Seth remembered, often in the quiet hours after a hard day, a song his mother used to sing to him. In this setting full of death and hardship, he looked up the words to the song and realized they were from Scripture: "The steadfast love of the Lord never ceases; his mercies never come to an end; they are new every morning; great is your faithfulness" (Lamentations 3:22–23).

Those words, written in the middle of Israel's ruin, reminded Seth that even in wreckage, God is still good. With that song of unending faithfulness in their hearts, Seth and Rebecca began together to see lament differently. It wasn't weakness or doubt to lament. No, crying out to God in pain, naming what was wrong, and acknowledging the ache of a broken world was worship.

It meant walking so closely with God that what broke His heart would break theirs too. They started leaning into lament rather than trying to push it away. It made their prayers deeper, their marriage stronger, and their hearts more tender toward the people they were there to serve.

This practice—this willingness to name pain while holding fast to hope—was another preparation. Sorrow would come closer than they ever imagined. But by then, they would know what to do with it. They would know how to grieve honestly, cling tightly, and walk through suffering, not with answers but with trust.

THE BIGGEST LETTING GO

In 2018, the sickness started subtly. Their eldest daughter, Arwen, then ten years old, was experiencing symptoms that didn't make sense. They weren't alarming at first, but something felt off. Tests followed tests, and soon the word no parent wants to hear was spoken aloud: *cancer*. The diagnosis fell like a thunderclap before a storm.

As a family, they returned to the United States for further observation and treatment for Arwen. They prayed for healing. They rallied friends and family. They asked the Lord to intervene, to restore. For a while, it seemed like maybe He would. Arwen's body responded, and she stabilized. There was laughter in the house again and color in her cheeks.

But the reprieve was short-lived. The cancer returned, harder this time and more aggressive. Eventually, doctors began using words like *palliative care*. They had done everything they could.

Around that time, Arwen told her parents something that would stay with them forever. "I think this is my ministry," she said. "Maybe my calling is to suffer well and help others see Jesus through that."

She said it with the calm clarity of someone who had made peace with what lay ahead. Arwen believed that if her story could point even one person to Christ, it would be worth it. She wasn't afraid—not of death, not of pain. She only wanted to be faithful.

Seth and Rebecca made the difficult decision to return to Togo and forgo any further treatment in the United States. It was what Arwen wanted—to be back in the place that had become home, surrounded by the people and rhythms she loved. Their missionary team welcomed them with open arms, knowing full well what this season would likely hold. The people made space for their grief.

That year was both beautiful and brutal.

Arwen had a good stretch at first—months of energy and joy. She spent time with her siblings, laughed with friends, soaked in the life around her. But as her health declined, the family entered a slow, sacred season of saying goodbye.

Seth and Rebecca didn't hide anything from their children. They were intentional about honestly explaining things in age-appropriate ways. They didn't sugarcoat reality. "Your sister may not grow up," they said. "She may go to heaven before the rest of us. But we'll see her again."

Arwen made videos for each of her siblings—messages of love, encouragement, and faith. She reminded them to follow Jesus, to keep trusting even when it got hard to see what God was doing. Those videos have become treasures, glimpses of a sister who lived and loved with purpose.

There were nights filled with tears, long walks, late conversations, and moments when grief cracked open their hearts. But through it all, the family held on to the same hope they had always preached—that death is not the end, that Christ has conquered the grave, and that heaven is not a vague comfort but a real home.

In those final days, Seth and Rebecca kept showing their children what it means to lament with trust. They wept together. They asked hard questions together. But they always came back to the truth: *God is good. God is near. God keeps His promises.*

Letting go of Arwen was the hardest, holiest surrender of their lives. But in the midst of that surrender, they saw God, not in the way they once hoped—through a miraculous healing—but in a quiet, sustaining way. He held them. He wept with them. And He reminded them again and again that Arwen was not lost. She was home.

Rebecca remembered that bathroom prayer years earlier when baby Elora was in the hospital barely breathing. Back then, she said, "She's not mine; she's Yours."

Now with Arwen, that same surrender returned, but it ran deeper. It was not just a one-time release. It was a posture, a way of breathing through the pain.

Seth clung to Scripture like a lifeline. Lamentations 3:22–23 became his anchor: "The steadfast love of the LORD never ceases; his mercies . . . are new every morning." He repeated those words to himself as a declaration of truth when the grief choked out everything else. He wasn't trying to be strong; he was just trying to be faithful and walk through that painful season with integrity.

Arwen passed away in February 2022. She was just fourteen years old.

The loss split their hearts wide open. But even in the pain, they could feel the presence of God—near, steady, unchanging.

Their home looks different now. One seat is always empty. One voice is missing from the laughter. But the Mallays don't live in despair. They live with open hands. They live with the knowledge that even their deepest sorrow has been caught up in the hands of a faithful God.

They had discipled their children through years of missionary life—through fear, change, and cultural transitions. But this—walking them through the death of a sibling—was something deeper. And yet the kids amazed them. Each grieved differently. Some asked questions, and others just wanted to be held. All of them in their own way pointed back to hope. They talked about heaven not as a vague comfort but as a real place.

Arwen's death didn't destroy their faith; it deepened it. They didn't walk away from God. They walked toward Him—limping, yes, but still moving forward, trusting that the God who gives also receives, and that even in loss, He is good.

GRIEF DOESN'T HAVE TO BE SOLITARY

In the darkest season of their lives, Seth and Rebecca discovered something unexpected, that grief can be lonely, but it doesn't have to be solitary. When they returned to Togo with Arwen, knowing the cancer was terminal and knowing her time was short, they weren't met with fear or avoidance.

They were met with presence.

Their missionary team didn't just make room for their sorrow; they stepped into it with them. It wasn't grand gestures that sustained them. It was meals delivered without being asked. It was teammates showing up, staying close, and sitting in the ache without needing to fix it.

As Arwen's condition worsened, their compound became more than a place of ministry. It became a family bound together, not by shared preferences or personalities but by shared pain and shared hope.

Living in such close quarters—walking distance from other team members, raising kids together, worshiping side by side—created a rhythm of daily life that made community not just convenient but essential. In the United States, grief might have been hidden behind closed doors or scattered across disparate schedules. But in Togo, it was witnessed, shared, and carried.

Seth and Rebecca's honesty about their journey broke down

any personal barriers because there was no pretense or spiritual gloss. Their friendship meant raw faith and fragile hope.

In the presence of others, something beautiful happened: unity. It was not the kind that comes from avoiding conflict or pretending everything's fine, but the kind forged in fire. It was the kind that can only come when people choose to suffer together and in doing so, remember Christ.

Their team mourned Arwen as if she were their own. And in many ways, she was. They had watched her grow, prayed for her healing, and then stood at her graveside together. The bonds formed in that season didn't fade with time; they deepened. Their shared grief became a shared testimony, a kind of unspoken agreement that *we carry each other because Christ has carried us.*

That kind of community doesn't just happen. It's built through honesty, held together by grace, and made holy by suffering. Seth and Rebecca didn't walk alone, and because of that, they didn't fall apart. Their team, unified around the gospel, became living proof that shared sorrow, when rooted in Christ, becomes not just bearable but sacred.

LAMENT IS A PRACTICE

If there's one thing Seth and Rebecca have learned, it's this: Everything in this world is temporary. The comforts, the dreams, even the people we love most—we are not to hold any of them tightly. And strangely, that truth has not made the Mallays bitter. It has made them free.

Letting go is something they've learned to embrace, and it's woven into the fabric of their life. They live a constant rhythm of surrender, trust, and worship.

They still grieve.

They still miss Arwen every single day.

But they don't live with fists clenched around the blessings in their lives. Instead, they live openhanded, knowing that Christ—not comfort—is their true reward.

Lament, for them, has become a life-long practice. So has unity. So has surrender. They know that faithfulness doesn't mean avoiding pain. It means trusting God with it, again and again.

Their story includes loss, but it's *about* joy and hope. As of this writing, Seth and Rebecca are still serving in Togo, still raising their kids in community, and still opening their home and hearts to others. They laugh. They celebrate. They look for and find signs of God's goodness in the ordinary. Their ministry is vibrant, not in spite of their grief but because of how God has met them in it.

They long for the day they'll see Arwen again. That hope is real, and it softens the edges of their sorrow. But they're not stuck in the waiting. They're walking forward, eager to keep saying yes to whatever God asks because the deeper their surrender, the lighter their load. And the more loosely they hold the things of this world, the more joy they find in what truly lasts.

What they've learned is simple but sacred: When you give everything to Jesus—even the things you never thought you could—you don't lose your life. You find it.

MY TAKE: FAITH EVEN IN SORROW

I remember walking with Seth and Rebecca through these extremely difficult days. I followed their updates closely, prayed for them all the time, and hoped with them for a turnaround.

And then I faced the unthinkable with them—Arwen wasn't going to recover. There's always that moment in situations like that when you realize the miracle you've been praying for isn't coming, and it's devastating. There's a perfectly natural temptation to ask, "Where are You, God?" But even in the heartbreak, you can see God's presence all over this story. His nearness brought such comfort even when the outcome wasn't what any of us wanted.

What really strikes me is Seth and Rebecca's sense of calling. They embody a depth of commitment that allows them to persevere even in great sorrow. Their daughter's desire to be buried in Togo speaks volumes. She caught that commitment from her parents, and that kind of legacy and generational impact is powerful.

Their story also reveals the beauty of community. As painful as this was, Seth and Rebecca weren't alone. They were surrounded by people who stood with them, supported them, and grieved with them. That's a testament to the kind of relational depth that's built when missionaries live fully invested in their communities.

I'm reminded again of the hardship and sacrifice that come with healthcare missions. Serving in these places is deeply costly. And yet the perseverance of people like Seth and Rebecca shows us what obedience, faith, and calling really look like, even when it comes at the highest personal price.

CHAPTER 7

LETTING GO WHEN A SEASON ENDS

DAN AND HEATHER GALAT

Dan Galat stood in the doorway of the Upper Room, hands on his hips, eyes scanning the space. Months earlier he and his wife, Heather, had dreamed up the space together. Heather had talked through colors and furniture while Dan sketched floor plans.

They wanted to build a guesthouse that would be a refuge for visiting surgeons, missionaries passing through, and young medical residents coming to Kenya to learn. The Upper Room would be an open space for prayer, meals, worship, and quiet. Dan imagined long conversations with windows cracked open to the breeze. The upstairs space would be a place to receive and be received, and serve those who served others.

Now an orthopedic surgeon, Dan had grown up on job sites, working alongside his dad in the thick dust of construction. Wood, concrete, and the hum of tools were all familiar to him. So even now, decades later and continents away, the building of this space in Kenya had been like a return to his childhood in Ohio. He worked closely with Kenyan builders and a very special project manager named Gimay who understood the vision like it was part of him. They built together slowly, lining up boards and building up walls. Gimay and the team worked while Dan supervised his vision coming to life before his eyes.

Heather had made the place warm, thinking about where the kettle would go, how to make the beds comfortable, and what kind of wall art might lift up a tired spirit. Between the two of them, the hoped-for place of rest and refuge came together. The Upper Room was both beautiful and useful. It represented hospitality, healing, and a vision for something that could last.

By the time the last shelf was stocked and the final curtain was hemmed, Dan was filled with that rare kind of peace that comes from knowing he had poured out everything and held nothing back.

What he did not know as he stood there that day was that six months later, he and Heather and their family would leave it all behind. They would leave Kenya and step into the unknown once again, following God's direction but also wondering if maybe they were walking out of their chapter before it was finished.

TRUE TOGETHERNESS

Heather never expected to meet her future husband on the way to a mission trip in Brazil. They found each other on the first leg of the trip, a bus ride to Miami, Florida. Upon arriving in South America, they worked in separate locations but reconnected at a church camp to talk about their labor abroad.

Heather had grown up surrounded by a family devoted to the church and the Christian faith but with little knowledge of medical missions. Her father's adventurous spirit and curiosity about the global church led to Heather going on several short-term missions trips during her teen years.

Then Dan showed up. He was kind and focused. When he talked about faith, he meant it, and his depth caught Heather off guard.

As they got to know each other, something settled in Heather's heart, and she realized Dan fit into the vision she had always had for her life, one of service and adventure.

When they got married a few years later, becoming missionaries wasn't the plan, but living radically was. They just didn't know what or how. They were young, idealistic, and deeply sincere.

While in seminary, Dan narrowed his focus and answered the call to medical missions. Heather agreed. She loved language, culture, and people. She imagined working alongside Dan in a local community, mentoring women and maybe starting a ministry of her own.

They forged ahead, and their life together took on its own momentum.

Seminary turned into medical residency. One baby turned into four. Somewhere in the middle of it, Dan fell in love with orthopedics—the tools, the structure, the way broken things could be put back together.

Dan and Heather talked often, especially in the early days, about where God was calling them to serve. Dan felt drawn to places where the need was great, and Heather was open and hopeful. It felt right to be aiming for something more significant than more money and more comfort. They both wanted to live poured-out lives and go where others wouldn't. They wanted to raise their kids with a sense of purpose.

Looking back, Heather can see how tightly they held to that shared calling. It steadied them and gave them direction. There was unity and true togetherness. They were building something they both believed in, and for a while, that was more than enough.

What they didn't realize was that they were aligned, but they hadn't yet been tested by exhaustion, resentment, or the isolation that comes when one person thrives and the other slowly fades.

That part was still coming.

THE MYTH OF THE LEAP

When they landed in Kenya in 2008, it felt like stepping into a dream they had carried for years. The red soil and the buzz of the motorbikes were everything they had pictured. Their kids were young, and the whole family took it in with a sense of wonder and excitement. The family piled into a borrowed van and drove through the hills to Tenwek where a modest house awaited them.

Dan hit the ground running. The orthopedic cases were constant—compound fractures, clubfoot repairs, late-stage infections that would've been handled weeks earlier anywhere else. There were barely enough hours in the day. The need was urgent and real, and Dan knew exactly what to do. He was in his element.

Heather tried to keep pace, but it was a different kind of race raising four kids in a developing country. She was homeschooling, managing the house help (which felt more like running a small business), and figuring out how to feed her family without the amenities she was used to in America. It all hit at once, and she felt the burden of little eyes watching how she adapted.

There was no rhythm and simultaneously no margin for error. Though she smiled for visitors and hosted dinners to keep the wheels turning, something inside her began to fray.

She tried to ignore the pressure that was building. They had trained for this, after all. They'd taken courses, read books, and been told to expect culture shock and spiritual warfare. Heather remembered nodding along, thinking, *We'll be fine. We've prepared.*

But no one had warned her about the slow, invisible kind of unraveling happening inside her. It happened not from a big crisis but from a thousand quiet disappointments.

Dan kept pushing forward. He wasn't blind to the strain Heather was under, but the mission felt too big to pause. The need was everywhere, and for the first time in his life, he felt completely, undeniably useful. He was helping people, training residents, and building something that would outlive him. His work mattered, and that kept him going.

As the days, months, and years went on, Heather felt stuck in a loop. Her days were spent over math books and spelling drills, refereeing squabbles between siblings, and navigating language and cultural barriers with staff. There was no time left for the ministry she'd imagined she'd do. There was no room to engage the community in any real way that mattered.

"I felt like I was just doing what I'd do in the States," she said later, "but with way more stress and a lot less support."

The bitterness crept in slowly, a dull ache that settled in her chest. She didn't resent Dan's work—she truly believed in it. But she resented how purposeless she felt. Their shared calling began to feel lopsided.

But they kept going because that's what missionaries do, right? They adapt. They tell themselves it's just a season.

In 2014, Dan launched a Pan-African Academy of Christian Surgeons (PAACS) orthopedic residency program at Tenwek. It was the first of its kind in Kenya and a major milestone that had been years in the making. Dan poured himself into the young African doctors, shaping a future that felt bigger than any single surgery. It was beautiful, but the cost to his family and marriage was high.

Heather tried to talk about it. Sometimes she hinted at the weight she was carrying and the anxiety she couldn't quite name, which leaked out in various ways to her family. But Dan was tired, too, and also deeply convinced that if they just kept going, God would meet them in the doing.

He truly thought that because they had jumped off the cliff—taken the initial leap of faith and obedience—that God would take care of the rest.

But the leap alone was not enough. It did not fix what was happening between them. On paper, everything looked successful. They had launched the program and treated patients, and their children were growing. But behind closed doors, they were two people whose leap of faith had landed them on different sides of a widening gap with their children sounding the alarm.

They had come to Kenya with one calling, but they were leading two very different lives.

THE CRISIS OF CALLING

They used to say it out loud like a family promise: *We'll stay as long as God keeps the door open.* That saying gave Dan and Heather peace and allowed them to release control without letting go of conviction.

For a while, the door stayed wide open—wide enough for their calling and their family. But they began to see signs that made them wonder.

When it came time for their oldest child to begin high school, he asked to go to a boarding school for missionary kids. Several of his friends were going, and though Heather had misgivings, she knew she couldn't continue to homeschool him properly through high school. So they agreed to send him to school three hours away from Tenwek. When he came home on breaks, he was quieter than usual, withdrawn, and sometimes edgy. Heather noticed it first, how he didn't talk about his dorm and seemed negative and angry about something. Dan thought maybe it was normal teenage stuff, but Heather knew it was a symptom of something deeper.

During that time, their oldest daughter, Emma, began her own battle while she was away at boarding school. Her experience included a group of girls who struggled with body image and at times had "mean girl" mentalities. Coupled with tension from home, Emma began a destructive journey with anorexia that completely overwhelmed her. She asked to come back home. She said she couldn't handle it alone anymore and that the emotional load was too heavy. Heather and Dan responded quickly, pulling her from the dorm and bringing her home. Unfortunately, the damage had taken root. Anxiety about the experience would take years to name, and the eating disorder would take years to heal.

Heather had managed to push down her own struggles, but seeing her kids this way was another thing altogether. She started asking the hard questions: *What are we expecting of our kids? What kind of faith calls you to serve while your family quietly suffers? What are we doing?*

Dan wanted to believe it was just a season and that things would even out. He felt that pushing through this hardship was an act of faithfulness. He had worked so hard to get there, built so much, and given so much of himself. Surely God wouldn't let it fall apart.

By the time they left for furlough in 2015, they were worn thin and running on fumes. Furlough was supposed to be a time of rest, but it turned into a reckoning.

While in the States, Dan took on temporary shifts as a traveling doctor to keep up their support. He was on the road for weeks at a time. Heather was back under her parents' roof with six kids, trying to figure out how to breathe again.

They were both grieving something they couldn't quite identify. Counseling sessions peeled back years of pressure and silence. The things they didn't make space to say at Tenwek finally surfaced, including Heather's isolation and growing resentment, the children's trauma at the boarding school, and the longing in Dan's heart that never quite left once he was back in America. The truth was, they had come to a crossroad in their calling.

Returning to Tenwek wasn't an option because their daughter was not well enough to go to boarding school. And for Dan, choosing to leave the hospital to move to a better location for the family felt like a betrayal. How could he leave? He had launched the PAACS orthopedic residency, discipled young doctors, and poured himself out in ways his family didn't get to see. Leaving felt like failure—like leaving something unfinished.

They remembered their own words: *We'll stay as long as God keeps the door open.* The door seemed to be closing. It had not slammed shut, but slowly and steadily the opening was narrowing. They had to discern—what was God calling them to do?

By the end of the furlough, they had made the difficult decision to return to Africa, but they would move from Tenwek to Kijabe, which was not the same as Tenwek. It was more established and more resourced. Most importantly, it allowed their kids to attend school as day students instead of being homeschooled or going to boarding school. The pressure eased, and Heather felt air in her lungs for the first time in years.

Meanwhile, Dan grieved in silence. At Tenwek, he had been needed. At Kijabe, he was useful but not essential. The shift was disorienting, and he struggled with feelings of pride and humility.

The transition to Kijabe didn't solve everything, but it did make room for their marriage to begin healing. It allowed them to pause their sprint in case they were running a race that God hadn't assigned them. The leap of faith they'd made years ago carried them far, but it was in slowing down and letting go that they started to see God's mercy.

Their calling hadn't ended. It was just changing shape.

WHEN CLOSURE DOESN'T COME

In 2019, Dan and Heather returned to the States for a year of training for Dan—a fellowship year to update his skills and stay sharp in new medical practices. They left all their personal belongings in storage with every intention of returning to Kijabe. That fellowship year was just a pause.

Somewhere in the middle of that year, between Dan's long shifts and the kids settling into American schools, it became clear. They weren't going back. It wasn't a decision that came from a big talk or one specific thing. Rather it was a slow revelation like fog lifting before their eyes.

Dan struggled with it deeply. The call to missions in Kenya had been strong. The fruit was very visible. But as he prayed and processed their situation, the weight of everything the family had been through came into sharper focus. And in this stillness, Heather started to realize just how much anxiety she was carrying and how she had ignored her own limits as a household manager and a homeschooling mother. The warning signs had been there for years, but she just kept hoping they'd go away if she tried hard enough.

At the time of this writing, the Galat family is still in America. Dan currently runs a solo orthopedic practice in Arizona where the family has integrated into the community. Their older children have since healed from their traumas at boarding school and are now married with their own children. Heather and Dan's younger children are still in school and living at home. The family has adjusted well to the pace and lifestyle of American culture.

But Kenya is still with them. Dan travels back when he can to teach and stay connected to the residents he helped train. Heather supports from home, advocating, praying for, and helping others who are preparing to go. Together, she and Dan also provide financial support for other missionaries, extending their impact far beyond their own reach. Their calling has become focused on equipping others and discipling their children. God's call and purpose for their lives haven't disappeared; they just no longer need a foreign address to feel valid.

There are still days when it aches in their hearts, especially for Dan—the unfinished work and the people he didn't get to say goodbye to, the guesthouse and Upper Room. He sometimes wonders if he'll ever stop feeling like something was left mid-sentence. But Heather sees it a little differently. Maybe some chapters are meant to stay unresolved for the next characters in God's story to finish out.

What's clear to both of them is that obedience isn't always about staying. Sometimes it's knowing when to leave. And when the ending isn't clean, purpose can still grow in the cracks. What Dan and Heather built still matters, and what they lost shaped them into the people they are today. Most of all, what they've learned is still unfolding, even now.

GOD WRITES THE STORY

The guesthouse and Upper Room are still there. Others stay in it now—residents passing through, visiting doctors, people Dan and Heather have never met. The dishes might be different, and the couch pillows might have been replaced by now, but the space remains—a quiet room above the guesthouse built for prayer and rest. It's being used—just not by Dan and Heather.

Sometimes Dan thinks about it in the middle of a long clinic day between back-to-back surgeries and notes on patients. He pictures the stairs he designed and the door frames he helped build. There's still a small part of him that aches to be there, not just in Kenya but in that lifestyle filled with fruit from daily labor. He didn't get to finish what he started, but he knows that's not the whole story. It's just a piece of it.

That Upper Room, the PAACS program, life in Kenya, and the whole season were never about outcomes. They were all about obedience and showing up with all they had. Even if Dan and Heather didn't stay long enough to see it all bloom, they have peace knowing they planted seeds when they were asked to.

They still talk about going back, maybe when the youngest of their now seven kids leaves for college, maybe when the doors open again—and not just logistically but in their hearts. Until then, they give in other ways—teaching, advocating, listening to younger families on the cusp of their own callings and telling them the truth both about what it cost and what it gave them.

The Galat guesthouse and Upper Room taught them that sometimes you build things you won't live in. Sometimes you plant seeds you'll never see sprout. But it all matters because God takes unfinished things and keeps writing the story.

MY TAKE: LIVING WITH OPEN HANDS

Though Dan and Heather are no longer living and working in Kenya, Dan's clinical work as an orthopedic surgeon and the developer of orthopedic surgery training programs left a legacy in that country that is still being felt today.

As impactful as his work was, the cost to their family was heavy. The fact that they went back to Kenya a second time tells you a lot about their commitment. Most people, after the kind of challenges they faced, wouldn't have gone back. Yet they did, believing it was the right answer at the time for their family. Eventually, though, they reached the point of discernment that every missionary dreads: the realization that it is time to return home. And sometimes that's exactly the right decision.

I resonate with this struggle. There's a painful tension between stepping into a calling and then sensing that God is asking you to step out of it. When I stepped away from pastoring, it felt like defeat even though I knew in my spirit that it was the right move. The surrender was real, and it hurt. I wrestled with the same question I imagine Dan and Heather faced: Is this failure, or is this obedience? Sometimes we fight the Spirit's nudge to move on because we don't want to give up on what we've invested in so deeply.

But God often has something else in mind that we can't see in the moment. For me, leaving the pastorate led to a broader impact through MedSend. In Dan's case, he continues to shape global healthcare missions through his leadership and mentorship.

The other layer in Dan and Heather's story is the impact their calling had on their children. I can only imagine how heavy it must have been to leave, knowing that the ministry needs were still great but also recognizing that their family's well-being had to take precedence.

I don't think that's failure. I think it's living in obedience with open hands, trusting God with the next step even when your heart is still conflicted. I think real faith lives in the tension of being willing to go but also being willing to leave when God says it's time.

CHAPTER 8

HOLD WHAT YOU'RE GIVEN

JUSTIN AND OLIVIA HOFFMAN

Justin never thought a cheap flight to Texas would change his life.

It was a spontaneous idea. He and his best friend, both in their final year of physical therapy school, had a week off between clinicals. For years they had watched an online Christian worship service streamed from a church in Texas every Tuesday night, ever since Justin's junior year of undergraduate studies in the Midwest. With an open week to do whatever they wanted, they decided it was time to see this ministry in person. So they booked the cheapest tickets they could find, packed lightly, and flew down to Texas to catch one of the services.

What they didn't know was that Olivia, an old friend of Justin's best friend, was also in Texas at the exact same time, finishing up a physical therapy clinical in San Antonio. It had been a couple of years since Olivia and Justin's buddy had seen each other, but when she saw his social media post saying he was at the Riverwalk in downtown San Antonio, she messaged him. The timing was too perfect not to meet up.

When Olivia joined them the next evening, Justin wasn't expecting anything beyond a casual hello. But something deeper began to unfold. He and Olivia found themselves talking about short-term mission trips to places like Guatemala and Africa. They talked about the moment they both realized there were people in the world who might live and die without ever hearing the name of Jesus. And they talked about how both of them were drawn to care for the vulnerable, about how they had both wondered what it might look like to take their skills overseas.

The conversation lingered in both their minds, even while Olivia stayed in Texas and Justin flew back to school at the end of the week. Despite the distance, they kept talking.

One year later, they were engaged.

GETTING CLEAR ON THE WHY

From the outside, their story might have looked like a whirlwind, but actually, each of them had been walking this path long before they ever crossed it together.

Olivia had grown up in a United Methodist church, the kind with regular youth group meetings and Sunday services. Her love for serving others started early through church trips, volunteer work, and a natural tendency to lean toward people in need.

College stretched her faith, pulling her through some drifting years until she came out on the other side with a faith that was her own. She went to a Jesuit university where service was part of the DNA, and even though she didn't take full advantage of the opportunities there, she found herself increasingly pulled toward something more.

During physical therapy school, she signed up for a medical trip to Guatemala. She still remembers the peace that settled over her while she was working in a makeshift clinic. It was hot and crowded, and the work was simple and hands-on. Something about it felt right, like the work she was made to do had finally found its place.

Justin had grown up going to church, but his faith didn't really become his own until college. It was through a campus ministry that the dots finally connected. And for the first time, he heard someone talk about entire regions of the world where people had never even heard the name of Jesus. It was a simple idea that stayed with him, that someone could live their entire life without access to the Gospel. It convicted him deeply.

Around the same time, he was narrowing in on physical therapy as a career. The field combined everything he was passionate about. His heart had always been drawn to kids with special needs, something he'd known even back in high school when he volunteered at adaptive swim programs.

By the time he met Olivia toward the end of physical therapy school, the foundation was already in place. His calling was growing, and meeting her was like finally finding someone who spoke the same language of service. They didn't have to convince each other. They didn't have to catch each other up. From their first conversation, they were already speaking from the same passion.

And still, they were young. They got married but didn't jump into long-term service overseas right away. Instead, they listened to wise counsel—mentors, pastors, and older couples they respected—who encouraged them to stay put for a while. They were told to grow their marriage and their clinical skills and serve together locally first. It was good advice.

For the next seven years, they worked side by side in the States. They got licensed, held jobs in hospitals and clinics, and learned to navigate adult life and marriage at the same time. They joined a church and began to lean into local ministry opportunities. The more they served, the more their calling clarified. They didn't know yet where they were going, but they were starting to get clear on *why* they would be going.

THE THREE CORE PASSIONS

Justin and Olivia's church was a rare kind of place, one where global missions was a focus and many workers were sent out. They took advantage of a perspectives class that provided a theological understanding of missions and how to directly apply the Great Commission. It opened their eyes to what being on the field could be like.

They also began volunteering with refugee families who had recently resettled in their city. They helped the children with homework, practiced English with them, visited homes, and simply listened. The more time they spent with those families, many of whom were from war-torn or underresourced areas, the more they began to see the intersections of their passion, their training, and their faith.

As they considered overseas ministry, their pastor told them to pray and be very intentional about what God had put into their hearts. What were their personal passions and interests? Over time, they clearly identified three things:

- **Refugees:** They had sat with families who had lost everything and still welcomed them in for tea during their tutoring sessions. They were able to see firsthand the confusion and courage it took to start over in a new country.

- **People with disabilities:** Through their work as physical therapists, both of them had seen how often people with disabilities were overlooked, misjudged, or hidden. In many cultures, people with physical or cognitive disabilities are kept out of view due to shame. That really grieved both Justin and Olivia, and they recognized the extra stigma and challenges this population faced within specific cultures.

- **The unreached:** They were burdened for those who, not by choice but rather by geography and culture, had never heard the gospel. This had been stirring in Justin's heart since college, and the more he and Olivia prayed together, the greater their conviction grew.

Together, these three passions—these burdens—formed a compass. Justin and Olivia didn't know yet where it was pointing, but it kept them moving forward.

A SEASON OF WAITING

By 2019, Justin and Olivia felt like everything was lining up. They had the training, the heart, the experience, and the support of their church. They'd identified the kinds of people they felt most called to serve. In every measurable way, it felt like the time to go had come.

They registered for the Global Missions Health Conference in Louisville, Kentucky, that fall, and they expected confirmation. They wanted doors to open, connections to fall into place, and someone to say, "Yes, you're the ones we've been looking for."

Instead, they left that conference with a message neither of them had expected: *Wait*.

It was a subtle and shared sense that God wasn't releasing them yet. Olivia describes it as something she felt in her spirit, a quiet "not now." For Justin, it became a conviction. "Whatever you're struggling with now," he sensed the Lord saying, "will only be magnified when you're overseas."

Deep down, Justin knew exactly what that meant: He had to learn how to process his anxiety. It wasn't new. It had been part of Justin's story for years. He had learned to manage it, mostly by pushing forward, keeping busy, and staying productive. From the outside, he looked steady, calm, and focused. But inside, it was a different story.

When Justin was stressed, he tended to overthink everything; his mind never fully turned off. He wasn't quite at a breaking point, but the issue was unresolved, and going overseas wasn't going to fix it. It would only make the issue heavier. A cross-cultural transition, unfamiliar systems, pressure to perform—all of those things would only push his anxiety to the surface and maybe, eventually, to a breaking point.

So instead of boarding a plane after the conference, they began to book counseling appointments. They started the inner work that most people try to avoid: a slow and vulnerable process of healing. None of it happened quickly, but it was all necessary to be healthy enough so Justin could pour out to others in the way he wanted to.

Looking back, both Justin and Olivia can see how mercy showed up in that delay. If they had launched too early, they would have carried unspoken expectations, invisible wounds, and some unhealthy patterns into a context that would only magnify those issues. But instead, they were given the gift of a pause, almost like a divine time-out that told them they weren't done being refined yet.

Justin started to make some progress and found himself able to more readily process his anxiety when it hit.

But then, just like that, the whole world shut down. Four months after the conference and just a few months into Justin's therapy, COVID hit the scene. Borders closed and international flights were halted. Business offices went remote. What seemed like a personal delay on their part had now become a global one.

But because Justin and Olivia were already in a season of pause, they didn't unravel over the circumstances. They settled into what God had before them. They used the lockdown season to lean deeper into their local work with refugees, and they got more involved with their care team and sending church. In that season, they had two babies and spent time learning how to be parents.

They decided to stop asking God, "When will we go?"

Instead, they began to ask, "How do we keep saying yes until You tell us to move?"

After that long life pause and with a clear headspace, they began talking again to their church's missions team. This time, they didn't have a sense of urgency but one of readiness. They weren't the same couple they had been just a year or two earlier. And in some ways, that was the whole point.

LETTING A SEASON TAKE ROOT

When the green light finally came, they had a united confidence that it was the right time for both of them. The waiting had done its work, and the next step was right in front of them.

They interviewed with a few organizations. After agreeing on one, they were offered nine locations to consider. They narrowed them down to three, ultimately choosing one location in the Middle East. It was home to thousands of refugees and had a growing need for disability services, and most importantly, there was already a small, faithful network of people doing the kind of work they hoped to join.

So they packed their things, said their goodbyes, and boarded a plane with their two young kids, a thousand unknowns waiting on the other side.

When they landed, they expected to feel disoriented. Everything around them was unfamiliar: signs written in Arabic, dry heat, the clamor of taxi drivers calling out words they didn't understand. But that feeling never came. Instead, it felt almost normal, like the place had been waiting for them. Despite the challenges that came that first year, one thing never left them—an inner peace from God that they were right where they were supposed to be.

They spent the first two years learning Arabic. Five days a week they sat in classrooms with audio recordings, wordless books, vocabulary cards, and tutors, learning how to communicate and figure out the cultural nuances of the area. There were no patients to treat.

It was humbling. Back home, they were experienced physical therapists with people who trusted them with complex cases and treatment plans. In this new home, they were barely surviving conversations at the market. Language school made them feel like toddlers again. They went from being confident and capable doctors to just trying to order coffee without completely failing.

They didn't realize it then, but it was another gift from God.

This language immersion gave them space to learn and understand culture not just through books but through neighborhood life and friendships. They learned how locals expressed grief, how they celebrated, how family worked, and how everything in this part of the world was spiritual. Faith was woven into everyday life.

In the West, politics and religion tend to be taboo topics in casual interactions. In their new surroundings, the name of God was on people's lips all the time as part of a normal greeting, a blessing, or discussions of the events of the day. Justin and Olivia found that they didn't have to wait for the perfect opening to talk about spiritual things because the conversation was already happening.

Two years of nothing but language and a slow entry into a new culture had no wasted moments. They were essential for stripping away the Americanness about them and teaching them a posture of humility necessary in that culture (or any new culture). It taught them to enter the field as learners, not leaders. They learned to respect before rushing to help, and they learned, once again, to wait and let the season take root with a strong foundation.

ON A LIVING ROOM FLOOR

After two years of language study, Justin and Olivia didn't launch into formal jobs as much as they eased into the rhythm of life in the Middle East. Like most things on their journey, the work grew slowly. They began partnering with two nongovernmental organizations (NGOs) that were doing meaningful work in very different ways.

The first, located in the city, made prosthetic legs for children and adults with amputations. The team fit the prosthetics, customized them, and provided ongoing care. Then Justin and Olivia came in as physical therapists, focusing on improving strength, range of motion, balance, and overall long-term mobility. They wanted to help the patients reach their own mobility goals while helping them adjust to the new limb. Though they couldn't openly preach a sermon in the clinic, it was normal to pray over a patient.

The second NGO focused on rural areas, desert communities, and nomadic families without consistent access to medical care. Justin and Olivia drove long stretches into the desert, often visiting families who lived in tents or modest concrete homes. The work was less structured there. They did basic health checks, but the real reason they went was to find the people others didn't see. They asked around and listened for names about the one family someone knew that might have a child with mobility challenges.

Little by little, the referrals came, because when word gets around that someone is coming to help your child or elderly family member without shame, it spreads quickly. The need became overwhelming, but Justin and Olivia took it one visit at a time.

The biggest impact, the kind they cared about most, happened during those types of home visits. They loaded up a car with supplies, navigated roads full of speed bumps, and sat with families where they were. The visits were designed to follow up on treatment but were also gateways. Their medical work was the doorway to trust—a reason to sit down with the family, hear a story, and ask questions.

In a culture where shame still surrounds disability, the message landed deeply. In many households, especially in more rural communities, people with disabilities are hidden. It's something to be managed quietly—to be fixed but not seen.

When Justin and Olivia walked into those homes, they knelt on the floor with their patients, asked their names, looked them in the eyes, and gave them basic human dignities through normal conversation. They cheered them on as they took a new step with a prosthetic or finally got off the floor to sit in a wheelchair for the first time. Sometimes that one moment changed everything. It gave the parents a new way of seeing their child as someone worth noticing and celebrating.

Justin and Olivia's work with the NGOs was intentionally holistic. They cared about physical healing, but they also cared about the spiritual and relational health of each person involved. They knew explicit spiritual conversations had to be handled with wisdom, but they also knew that people notice when love shows up again and again without condition.

It turns out that their favorite moments in ministry happened on living room floors.

THE COFFEE CUP

There's a metaphor Justin and Olivia often turn to: the coffee cup.

When they were in the States, everything was big—their schedules, their responsibilities, their expectations. They both came from systems that rewarded full plates, packed calendars, and maximum output. Rest was a reward for productivity, or something you earned after checking off every item on your to-do list.

In the Middle East, the cups are smaller—literally.

Rather than oversized mugs, people drink coffee from tiny cups meant to hold just a few sips at a time. They drink slowly, talk between sips, and trust that more will come when it's needed.

That image has come to define more than just coffee for Justin and Olivia. It's a picture of their new pace and capacity for work—their new way of measuring faithfulness.

Especially in their first year, the coffee cup was a metaphor for their daily capacity. They found that they more quickly hit the bottom of their cups. And they did not always like the person they found at the bottom. God taught them to come to Him to fill their cups. In a new country and culture, they would accomplish less each day, and that was okay.

"We're not made to hold the whole pot," Olivia says. "We hold what we're given. And here on the field, that smaller cup is enough."

They've stopped chasing the American ideal of doing it all. They've learned to live inside their God-given limits, to value presence over productivity, and to rest without guilt and enjoy time with their now three children.

They still show up and work hard, but they know that living *poured out* doesn't mean living *burned out*. As they've come to learn, obedience usually looks like being still and waiting on the Lord. Sometimes calling looks like doing fewer things with deeper attention.

And sometimes faithfulness is just waking up, loving the people in front of you, and trusting God to refill the cup tomorrow.

MY TAKE: THE BLESSING OF WAITING

To me, Justin and Olivia's journey is a picture of patience. They were willing to wait on the Lord. They were willing to take a step back. They were willing to be vulnerable and take the time required to heal.

We live in a broken and fractured world. In my years of seeking the Lord and trying to understand how He works, I've come to the conclusion that no one gets through life without some level of brokenness. And whether we like it or not, that brokenness becomes part of our testimony. God uses it to teach us patience with ourselves, with those we love, and with Him as He works to restore us.

My personal experience is that anytime you wait on the Lord, the blessing is magnified. The waiting clears space for His plans to take precedence over our own. And in the waiting, Justin and Olivia were still seeking the Lord, asking, "How can you use us right where we are?" Instead of chasing their calling prematurely, that question led them to the refugee community and into deeper preparation for life in the field. They moved forward as a couple, trusting God to work out the timing.

In the Christian life, sanctification—the ongoing process of becoming more like Jesus—is a kind of waiting. The point is not to sit idly but to keep showing up and asking, "What can I do now, Lord, to serve Your purposes?" That posture may lead to the mission field, or it may lead to the person across the street. Either way, it's a beautiful act of obedience, and the fruit of that kind of patience can be both life-changing and God-honoring.

CHAPTER 9

YOU'RE ONLY AS STRONG AS YOUR TEAM

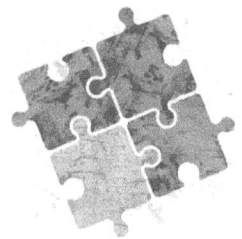

STEPHANIE AND ANDREW ONGUKA

T he email sat unopened for a few days before they forced themselves to read it.

Andrew and Stephanie,

We've gathered some of our own personal funds as a gift for you. Spend this money on a weekend away together. Fix what needs fixing in your relationship. Please take it. You need to be unified in marriage to be unified on the mission field.

Love,
Your Prayer and Care Team

Their eyes locked. Stephanie backed away from the computer screen, swept aside her blonde hair, and crossed her arms. "No way. We can't take their money. And besides, I don't even *want* to go away with you."

Never one to shy away from a difficult conversation, Stephanie spoke with conviction. As she reread the email, a flicker of emotion crossed her face—frustration, maybe even hurt—but she remained firm. The idea of using their friends' generosity for this reason didn't sit well with her.

Andrew knew this side of her well. It was part of what had drawn him to her in the first place. He had always admired the way she met a challenge head on. Over the years, their spirited conversations had become a familiar rhythm in their marriage. It was a dynamic that kept them both engaged.

But this time felt different. The message from their Prayer and Care (PAC) team hadn't just pointed out a disagreement; it had exposed something deeper. Their growing disconnection was no secret, but seeing it reflected back at him so plainly left Andrew feeling unsettled.

With a tired sigh, he decided to set the argument aside, at least for now.

This temporary disconnection with Stephanie would have to wait.

And so it did, for a time.

TWELVE YEARS BEFORE THE DRIFT

Andrew and Stephanie met in 2005. At the time, Andrew was a graduate student at Gordon-Conwell Theological Seminary in Massachusetts and about to begin an international mission. As a Kenyan, it seemed a little strange that he was headed back to his home country to complete an overseas practicum. But when the opportunity to educate Sudanese refugees in a refugee camp in Kenya presented itself, he jumped at the chance. As he stepped off the plane alongside the two female classmates he'd traveled with, he surveyed the rest of the group: two other men and a blonde woman who smiled right back at him when their eyes met.

He quickly found out her name: Stephanie, a bright-eyed American from Maryland. She was about to begin her third year of medical school at Georgetown University, and she had signed up to teach healing prayer on this particular trip. She shared with the group how her pastor had introduced her as a teenager to the world of international missions. Whether through medicine or prayer or both, she was committed to healing in all the ways she knew. Andrew was immediately drawn to her passion.

The group got to work and jumped into helping the refugees transition to a new country. Andrew found himself trying to get to know Stephanie every chance he got. At lunch, he sat across from her, and during group walks, he somehow found himself next to her.

Their connection was obvious and instant. Not only did they have similar, strong-willed personalities, but their individual convictions to serve God only deepened their attraction to each other. Despite their immediate surroundings, they both loved to laugh and make each other laugh. Andrew liked Stephanie's boldness, sharp mind, and relatability. He could easily see what a great doctor she would be.

As part of their mission experience, the group journaled about their daily insights and reflections. Andrew wrote this:

Stephanie asked me today why I wanted to come back to Kenya for this practicum and if I'd ever want to serve here in the future. I know I do. I know it doesn't make sense to my family, to be able to make it to America where money grows on trees just to turn around and come back home. But I have a heavy burden for the youth of my country. Stephanie encouraged me to follow my conviction. I like how she listens to me and allows me to be unapologetically myself. She doesn't try to push me to be something I'm not. She makes me feel proud to want to come back to Kenya.

With each nightly journal entry, it became more and more obvious that Andrew was growing fond of Stephanie.

One day, the mission team leader had a strange request. Somehow the conversation had turned to Christian marriage, and when some of the Sudanese refugees said they'd never seen one, their mission leader suggested that the team act one out. Andrew smiled as Stephanie played the bride, but when another teammate acted as the groom, he felt a twinge of jealousy. That sealed the deal—he liked her, and he wanted to tell her.

The practicum came to an end shortly after, and Andrew knew he had to do something before it was too late.

As they packed up their belongings from the dormitories, Andrew watched Stephanie prepare for her next adventure with the ladies from his seminary. She had plans to travel for a couple of weeks with them, hoping to experience a safari and the coast before returning home to the States.

Recognizing an opportunity, he boldly asked to join them at the coast. Stephanie met the idea of extending their time together with enthusiasm, making it clear that neither of them was ready to part ways just yet.

So Andrew joined Stephanie and the ladies on their travels, which culminated at the Peponi Hotel, an Arabic-inspired resort on the island of Lamu off the coast of Kenya. Their last night there, Andrew and Stephanie stayed up in the lounge talking so late into the night that they witnessed several calls to prayer. By dawn, Andrew had asked her for a proper first date. With the joy of starting a new relationship, Stephanie said yes.

Once they got back to Nairobi, Andrew planned their date to a giraffe center and a coffee house. He sipped his tea as Stephanie reflected on her path to medicine. She recognized her gift for healing and saw it as an opportunity to help those in need, a calling they both shared. However, her interests extended beyond medicine. Growing up near Washington, DC, had sparked a fascination with politics. She dreamed of one day serving as a health commissioner or even secretary of the U.S. Health and Human Services Department. Despite those ambitious goals, she remained open to whatever the future might hold, trusting that God's plan would unfold in its own time.

Grinning with this new information, Andrew grabbed a napkin off the table and began to draw a political tree and timeline—the Who's Who of Kenya, complete with stick figures and labels. Stephanie laughed at his clever attempt to connect with her passion for politics.

Inspired to share something deeply personal, Andrew decided to end the date at an unexpected location. For their last stop, he took her to a slum.

Andrew had spent much of his young adulthood ministering there—teaching, doing social work, and planting churches. The needs at this particular slum reflected his own impoverished childhood. As soon as he was in the position to help, he did. This slum was where his heart for his people had formed.

He knew it might seem a strange way to end their first date, but if Stephanie was really meant to be with him, she would likely feel the same way about the slums as he did. She jumped right in and felt at home, as he had suspected she would. She didn't seem bothered by the rows of homes that were falling apart, the ragged clothing, or the smells of rotten things. Together they gave hugs, stopped to pray when someone asked, and even joined in a round of pool with youth from a gang. Andrew's vision of a life of service began to include Stephanie as a life partner.

Less than six months later, they were engaged to be married.

SEVEN YEARS BEFORE THE DRIFT

After that first date, Andrew and Stephanie returned to the United States, and life went back to normal. They dated long distance for a year as they finished up their studies. Finally, they confidently moved into the season of marriage and settled into a new community in Lancaster, Pennsylvania. Stephanie began her residency in family medicine, and Andrew put his master's degree to use doing drug and alcohol counseling at a local mission for those struggling with life-controlling issues. But even as they engaged their community, they had a burden for Kenya—a conviction to serve the Kenyan people.

By God's providence, they became members of Calvary Church in Lancaster, a church with a heart for missions. Steve Beirn, the church's global ministries pastor, wrote the book *Well Sent* that focuses on how local sending churches can best support their missionaries. Calvary Church practiced what the book preached.

Before being commissioned and sent from Calvary, all missionaries were asked to choose a Prayer and Care (PAC) team. These teams prepare homes during missionaries' home assignments, cover bills such as groceries and utilities when needed, and even send monetary gifts for vacations so missionaries can take a break to recharge. They are the hands and feet of Jesus, supporting those serving abroad. And of course, they commit to praying for their missionaries.

When Andrew and Stephanie accepted a commission to Kenya—Andrew's native land and the place their relationship began—their PAC team surrounded them and prayed for their courage, provision, and unity.

Stephanie was in awe of how God had worked so masterfully at equipping them. Even though this decision meant she would be leaving behind her medical practice and her family in America, she didn't once question that God had planned this for her all along.

After all, it had been so easy to fall in love with Andrew in Kenya. She was awed by how much pride she took in being married to a man with such strong convictions to help his home country.

And with this PAC team who were committed to praying and caring for their needs as they boldly obeyed their calling, it was time to answer the call. It was time to move to Kenya.

THE DRIFT APART

For the fourth time, Stephanie looked out the window of their university faculty apartment in Kabarak, hoping to see Andrew's car pulling up.

He still wasn't home. She sighed unhappily.

"Boys, let's start eating dinner. I'm not sure when Dad will get home tonight," Stephanie called out to their three sons.

She lovingly watched them wiggle energetically into their seats around the table. She was always in awe of her miracle children. When she and Andrew first began their mission, she wasn't sure if she'd ever have children.

In the months before they left for Kenya seven years earlier, she and Andrew had been diagnosed with "unexplained infertility." The news had devastated her. All her life she had known she wanted to eventually become a mom. When the time came that they wanted to have kids, infertility was a horrible surprise that shocked her to her core.

In that season, Stephanie struggled with what it meant for her life and what it said about her worth as a woman, and especially a woman in the African context. This fear was only multiplied by mentally processing the move to a new country and starting a new life as a missionary doctor.

Andrew navigated the pain alongside her in the unique way only a husband could. He reminded her first and foremost that their family was complete with just the two of them and Jesus. He also reminded her of the dream they had shared when they met: adopting children. Embracing this path, they adopted their first son, Jonathan, in Kenya.

Two years later, just as they planned to adopt again, Kenya's laws changed, restricting adoptions to Kenyan citizens only. Though Stephanie had applied for Kenyan citizenship, delays made them uncertain about expanding their family. Miraculously, their paperwork was expedited, which allowed them to adopt their second son, Peter.

But God wasn't even close to being done with this miracle. One week before the adoption agency matched them with Peter, Stephanie tentatively took a pregnancy test. There were signs she could be pregnant, but so much heartbreaking disappointment had made her skeptical. Reluctantly, she tested and was shocked to see a positive result.

After years of infertility, they were finally expecting. Nine months later, she held both Peter and their biological son, Boaz, in her arms, declaring them her "twins" because they had grown together in her heart.

Stephanie looked at her children now as they sat at the dinner table without Andrew for the third time that week. She held tightly to her American belief that "a family who eats together stays together." Just the week before, she had argued with Andrew that this was the perfect time to connect on a daily basis. She wanted the routine of sharing one meal a day together to talk openly about everyone's day.

It wasn't that Andrew didn't want to connect with his family, but as a Kenyan, he struggled with the whole concept. In Kenyan culture, kids eat last. The family hierarchy is respected at mealtimes, and children rarely eat with their parents.

In addition, Andrew's heavy workload often continued into the evening hours. It just didn't make sense to stop his momentum for a shared meal that didn't hold significance for him.

Andrew was the director of OneLife Africa, a youth development program he had founded. The program's goal was to equip young people through mentorship, education, entrepreneurship, and community service, encouraging their growth in Jesus's name.

Andrew's heart was on fire for the mission, and he often stayed late if he was in the middle of mentoring a student or making plans with a building developer for the construction of a youth campus. He was doing exactly that as his family ate dinner without him yet again.

The boys were still too young to know that anything was wrong. Stephanie smiled tiredly, not wanting the kids to sense how frustrated she was and pretending that all was okay.

But she wasn't okay.

Taking care of three young boys was hard.

Taking care of three young boys while on the mission field was especially overwhelming.

After the "twins" came along, Stephanie had stepped back from her full-time role in medical education at the family medicine residency program she had helped launch at Kabarak University. In that season, she just didn't have the capacity to be full-time Dr. Stephanie and also full-time mom.

Stephanie felt alone and isolated at her post several hours from Nairobi. The days stretched long, filled with the demands of the tiny humans always crying out for her.

Stephanie didn't resent Andrew's absence—or at least she tried not to. He did good, important work that she believed in, but there were moments when the loneliness was suffocating. She wanted someone to acknowledge her sacrifice and hardship. She wanted to hear someone say, *I see you. You're not alone in this. You're worthy. You have a purpose, and that purpose is a great one for the Kingdom.*

She wondered, *Am I strong enough for this? Am I failing? Why does it feel like I am in this alone?*

The next day, Stephanie reached out to her American mentor of many years—someone who had been married decades longer than she and Andrew, and had lived in Kenya longer than they had. The friend invited Stephanie to stay with her a few days to connect with other girlfriends and for more honest conversations.

"He didn't come home for dinner again. I think I'm at my breaking point," Stephanie confessed.

"Just take some time apart from each other," her friend said. "If he doesn't see you for a while, he'll realize he misses you. Maybe tell him to move out and just stay at the OneLife campus until construction finishes. It might be good for your marriage."

Stephanie's heart sank at the advice. She was upset that Andrew wasn't around, so why would asking him to move out be the answer?

But she knew she couldn't keep living like this—alone and unheard. She needed prayer and discernment. Later that day, she sat down at her computer.

PAC Team Ladies,

I feel your prayers every day and could use some now. I may be asking Andrew to spend some time apart from us in order to get him to see what he is missing. My mentor gave me the idea to have him stay at the OneLife compound. I don't know if it's the right thing to do, but I can't keep going the way I have been. Please pray for our next steps.

—Stephanie

DRIFTING PARALLEL TRACKS

That email was what triggered their PAC friends to send the message that offered funds for a getaway. But instead of relief, Stephanie felt sadness. Her voice rang with raw truth and an underlying—maybe even undiscovered—regret when she told Andrew, "I don't even *want* to go away with you."

How would taking a vacation help them right now? Once they came home from their vacation, wouldn't their problems still be there?

The questions kept coming, and there were no answers. The days wore on, and then another email arrived in their inbox.

Stephanie and Andrew,

The money is here, just sitting. We're sending it to you. How do you want to receive it? Paypal? Venmo? Bank deposit?

—Your PAC Team

Stephanie finally responded:

Dear PAC Team,

Thank you from the bottom of our hearts for this money. I'm still not sure if going on a trip away will solve our problems, but we agreed to schedule something in the next few months. It's such a gift to know you all care and are praying for us.

—Stephanie

In the waiting, the questions kept coming.

Where did that passionate young couple go—the one ready to take on the world? The couple filled with purpose to heal the Kenyan people together? The couple who met duty and sacrifice with boldness and challenge?

Stephanie didn't know the answers to those questions, and as a result, she felt more alone than ever. She ignored a few of the texts, calls, and emails from the PAC women. She didn't know what else to say but was comforted by their prayers. She couldn't believe that the idea of separation from Andrew felt like a relief—not divorce, not the end of everything, but time apart.

Space to breathe.

Space to force Andrew to see.

The words landed like a stone on her chest. Was this where they were? Was she really at the point where stepping away seemed like the only way forward?

Stephanie imagined marriage as two people walking side by side, sometimes adjusting their pace but always moving in the same direction. She and Andrew had once been like that—partners, equals, deeply connected even in the chaos of life and ministry. But somewhere along the way, their paths started to shift.

Now they were two trains running on separate tracks, moving forward but no longer alongside one another. The tracks weren't even running parallel; they were diverging slowly and steadily without either of them meaning for it to happen. They were heading in different directions. It was the drift.

This wasn't just a rough season. It wasn't just stress. It was the quiet unraveling of everything they had built, and Stephanie wasn't sure how they would find their way back together.

They settled on a vacation destination a month or so later. Though the weekend away alone together was a nice break from caring for the children, it didn't erase the loneliness Stephanie felt, as she had suspected. It did ease it, though, as they took a small step in the right direction.

Back at home, nothing changed dramatically in their daily rhythm, and they continued to live what felt like separate lives. Still, Stephanie felt the Lord's blessing on this small act of obedience, and her heart softened a bit, perhaps easing resentment.

But that didn't change their reality. Andrew remained busy, and Stephanie remained isolated and alone.

THE PAC TEAM

Stephanie and Andrew's Prayer and Care team wouldn't let it go. They weren't the kind of people who just listened and moved on. They couldn't be. After all, it was for seasons like this in a missionary's life that the team had formed. They saw Stephanie's pain, heard what she wasn't saying, and then did something she never expected. They refused to let her stay stuck.

They kept checking in and reminding her that they were there. They saw what was happening and believed in her marriage even when she wasn't sure she did. The more they pushed, the more something inside her softened—not in a dramatic, sweeping way but in small, quiet moments.

It was the realization that these people loved her and Andrew enough to fight for their marriage when she was too tired to fight for it herself. It was the way they didn't shame her for struggling. They didn't act like she should just be stronger, more faithful, or more grateful. They simply stood in the gap, refusing to let her believe the lie that she was alone.

Then one day Stephanie received an email from Dr. Chris Hager, one of their PAC team members.

> *Stephanie,*
>
> *I have an idea that hit me last night, and it felt like a Holy Spirit moment. I hope it might become an answer to unsaid prayers. How would you feel about coming to America a few times a year to cover for me at my practice when I have vacation or other planned time out of the office? You'd act as my substitute and receive full payment for your time. Does this sound like something you'd like to do?*
>
> *—Chris*

Stephanie's heart jumped with excitement, far more than when the original PAC team offered money for a vacation with Andrew. This was different. Someone needed her and her medical experience. She felt a spark of purpose come alive in her heart, one she hadn't realized had dimmed in her break from actively practicing medicine.

Whether Dr. Hager knew it or not, his email was like a lifeline for Stephanie—and just maybe a lifeline for her marriage. It felt surreal, like someone had seen a piece of her she had long buried and held it out, reminding her of who she used to be.

For the last few years, she had been a doctor in title only. She had trained, sacrificed, and poured herself into medicine, only to set it aside when their mission work and family demands made it impossible to keep up.

She thought she had made peace with it. But somewhere along the way she had stopped feeling like herself. She had become Andrew's wife, the mother of three, the one who held everything together at home while everyone else moved forward.

But now, here was an opportunity to step back into something that had once given her life—to see patients again and engage with medicine. She'd feel useful in a way that had nothing to do with making lunches, managing meltdowns, or keeping a crumbling marriage from falling apart.

Stephanie shared the note from Dr. Hager with Andrew, her eyes bright with hope. He easily saw the excitement in her expression and immediately began considering how they might make the opportunity possible.

Stephanie didn't expect Andrew to resist, but she also hadn't expected him to support her the way he did. Part of her braced for a pushback, not because Andrew was unsupportive but because for so long their lives had been built around his work, his calling, and the weight of her responsibilities at home. She had already given up so much so their family and ministry could function. Would he really understand why she needed this?

He definitely did.

Maybe he recognized the exhaustion in her eyes or the way her spirit had dulled under the daily weight of parenting and isolation. Or maybe he knew deep down that if she didn't reclaim some part of herself, she would slip even farther away.

So he didn't just say yes; he *encouraged* her to go. He reassured her that their family would be fine without her for a little while. The boys would be okay, and he would step in. He made it clear that she was not being selfish. She deserved to do something that brought her life, something that reminded her of who she had been before everything became so heavy.

For the first time in a long time, Stephanie felt like someone was holding *her* up instead of the other way around.

GOD USES PEOPLE TO WRITE YOUR STORY

You're only as strong as the people around you. Hiding problems in isolation creates barriers, while opening up invites others to walk with you in love and support. Andrew and Stephanie's relationship is a testament to that belief.

There had been several seasons of drift when they felt like they were on separate paths, moving farther and farther apart with another move, developmental delays, and the difficulties of homeschooling on the mission field.

But the relationships—their own, the ones with their care team and faith community—always pulled them back together. Their PAC team didn't just offer support; they fought for Stephanie and Andrew when they were too weary to fight for themselves.

After eighteen years of mission work and marriage, Stephanie and Andrew can now look back in wisdom to share how God united them in times of struggle, loneliness, and tension.

Pay attention to the people who come your way. God will use them to write your story. It's about leaning on community, learning from others, and allowing God to work through every relationship to strengthen your bond. Through every challenge and every season, Stephanie and Andrew saw firsthand that a strong marriage isn't built alone. It's nurtured through faith, community, and the unwavering support of those who walk alongside them.

As Andrew and Stephanie continue their journey in Kenya, they do so with the certainty they are never alone. They're held together by the very relationships that have shaped their story.

MY TAKE: YOU HAVE TO BUILD YOUR TEAM

Stephanie and Andrew's story brought tears to my eyes. I've known them for a few years and have seen the amazing love they've poured into their work in Kenya. But I had not heard this story, and I did not know about their PAC team.

What an incredible gift! Imagine having a church so committed to caring for their missionaries that they *require* everyone to have a PAC team. Imagine having a team of supporters who over the years become friends who stand with you no matter what—friends who don't accept pat answers, friends who continue to care even when it's messy.

Unfortunately, many missionaries tell a different story. With bright-eyed enthusiasm and an eagerness just to get to the field, they seek out a sending agency and a sending church. The agency takes care of logistics and ministry details while the sending church sends them out with love and prayers. Other churches and individuals join in, sending monthly support checks and maybe an email every once in a while. And that might be about as deep as it gets. The intentions are good on all sides, but the truth is that it's hard to truly support someone you don't really know. And it's hard to be vulnerable with a group of people who are mostly strangers.

Or maybe the relationship starts off strong, but with time and distance, the ability to relate to one another becomes increasingly difficult. The prayer requests become more vague. The newsletter reports are more forced. Supporters move on to other ministries, content to send the monthly checks. It's all well-intentioned but fairly superficial.

Then, when missionaries return on home assignment seeking refreshment and rest, they walk into church after church only to find that they don't know anybody. They may recognize a face here and there, but a lot can change in a few years. And they just don't feel free to share the deep, difficult truth of what they're experiencing.

Supporters are interested, but they simply don't know what to say to get beyond the basics. They don't have any concept of the grinding, daily demands of ministering in intense, underresourced countries. Both parties suffer. Donors have no awareness of what's really going on, and the missionaries are not well cared for.

I know it sounds bleak, but it doesn't have to be this way. That's why Andrew and Stephanie's PAC team is so inspiring. That's why this story brought tears to my eyes. Thinking of all the missionaries who are struggling and feeling alone, I thought, *There's hope! This is a church that gets it!*

If you're preparing for the mission field, think about your team. You may feel invincible now, but who is in your corner? Who can you reach out to when the going gets rough? If your church doesn't have a structured support plan, you may have to create it for yourself. Be intentional. Find a few people you trust, and dial up the vulnerability now while you're optimistic and fresh.

And if you're on the field struggling, seek help. That is exactly why MedSend developed the Longevity Project. Whether it's counseling, a family retreat, or a visit from a friend, there are resources available. Let others help. Be vulnerable. Don't try to go it alone when you are struggling.

Supporters, lean in. Your missionaries appreciate your financial support, but they also need your prayers, your understanding, and maybe even your loving intervention.

The long-term commitment and level of transparency between the Ongukas and their team is remarkable. I'm guessing that Stephanie and Andrew were grateful for it from the beginning but only over time did they come to understand its true worth.

They could be authentic. They could admit that they were hurting and that their kids were struggling. They could confess that their marriage was in trouble. The team had earned that trust. Their team stepped up time and again.

And that made all the difference.

CHAPTER 10

CHOOSING A LIFE OF RECONCILIATION

MICHELLE AND ADAM YATES

Vines curtain the jungle, and Adam can't find the pathway. He grips the handlebars of his motorcycle as he hurtles through the tangle of leaves. Suddenly, arms squeeze around his waist, and he turns around in surprise. A passenger sits, grinning, behind him on the motorcycle.

It's Michelle, the woman he started dating two weeks ago. He really likes her. In fact, his heart beats faster knowing she is on this adventure with him. Her presence grounds him.

With newfound confidence, he twists the throttle. He's glad he's not riding solo. This journey is meant for both of them, wherever it leads.

Adam jolted awake, the motorcycle dream burning in his mind. As an engineer who relied on logic and calculated every decision, he had never put much stock in dreams. But something felt different about this one. It felt like a message, sharp and clear.

But *what* was the message, and *who* was sending it?

Up until that moment, Adam had imagined a stable future—a good job, a traditional marriage and family life, a comfortable and stable home—a lifestyle similar to his own childhood.

Michelle, the woman on the motorcycle with him, envisioned a different path. She had told Adam from their first conversation that she was going to be a medical missionary. Her calling was clear. Adam admired her conviction, but it also unsettled him to think of abandoning his structured future. Follow Michelle into the unknown? That wasn't part of the equation.

Yet the dream refused to fade, and in the dream, Adam didn't just follow Michelle into the jungle. He *belonged* there, right alongside her. For days, he wrestled with what this dream might mean.

Maybe his subconscious was processing doubts about continuing to date her.

Maybe he was overthinking.

But no matter how much logic he applied, the image of driving that motorcycle through the jungle wouldn't leave him. Somehow, God had placed it in his heart, breaking through his carefully constructed plans.

It finally dawned on Adam that this was about his purpose. God wanted him to surrender his own plans for a much greater one. Adam was called to something much bigger than himself.

And if Michelle was on that bike with him, maybe this wasn't just a fleeting romance. Maybe she was meant to be his partner in this calling.

With boldness, Adam told Michelle about the dream. "I think this means I can marry you," he said.

She stared at him, stunned.

To be fair, it was a lot to drop on someone after only three weeks. But Adam wasn't making a formal proposal; he was making a decision. He was saying yes, not just to her but to the possibility that life could look differently than he'd always imagined. And in that moment, his carefully laid plans felt small compared to the thrilling unknown God was unfolding before them.

MEN ARE JUST DISTRACTIONS

By the time Michelle went to college, she had mapped out her future with military precision—med school, family medicine residency, a life devoted to serving overseas as soon as she finished her studies. There would be no detours, especially not the kind that came with broad shoulders and charming smiles. She had seen it happen before—strong, determined women setting aside their dreams for a relationship—and she wasn't about to be one of them.

"Men are just distractions," she told her friends who tried to set her up on dates. So when a classmate insisted on setting her up with a "really nice Christian guy," Michelle dragged her feet before saying yes. The last thing she needed was a romantic subplot.

Adam, on the other hand, was actively looking for his leading lady. He had completed his engineering degree and started his career in the field. He jokingly asked friends to set him up with "hot Christian med students." He imagined meeting someone who shared his faith and values, someone he could build a stable, meaningful life with.

Adam never expected his blind date to be Michelle—fierce, passionate, and absolutely uninterested in adjusting her course for anyone.

"I'm going to be a medical missionary," she told him. "That's always been the plan."

She might as well have been waving a giant red warning flag.

But instead of Michelle's conviction scaring Adam off, it fascinated him. Michelle wasn't looking for a man to lead her or follow her. She was inviting someone to join her. And if that someone wasn't Adam, then she was fine with it.

Adam, who had always imagined a steady, structured life, suddenly found himself wondering what exactly he wanted. Was it a woman who fit into his plans or a woman who lived out God's plans? He had always seen his future very clearly, but now he wondered if God was nudging him toward something different.

Pleasantly surprised, Michelle found herself drawn to Adam's steady presence. He wasn't trying to change her course or talk her out of missions. He wanted to understand it. He wanted to support it.

Somehow, they both knew they were standing at the edge of something bigger than either of them imagined.

They got married a year and a half later.

CRACKS IN THE FOUNDATION

Saying yes to the mission field together was one thing. Getting there was a whole different battle. Michelle and Adam expected challenges, but neither of them anticipated just how many doors would slam shut as they tried to get overseas. It was hard to accept the nos when all they wanted to do was serve and help. They were ready to uproot their lives in America, but they were met with rejection after rejection.

The biggest blow came when they were turned down by a well-known missions fellowship program. It had seemed like the perfect fit: a structured path to the mission field, financial support, and a well-established network of missionaries. They had poured themselves into the application process, believing this was God's plan. When the rejection letter arrived, they couldn't believe it.

Were they not experienced enough?
Did they lack the right connections?
Had they misunderstood their calling?

They began to doubt themselves. If a program specifically designed to send medical professionals to the mission field didn't think they were ready, then who would?

With bruised egos, they kept pursuing God's calling over their lives. They turned to their home church—the one they had attended for several years during residency—and entered their sending process.

But just when they thought they were making progress, the pastoral staff of their sending church hit the brakes. Instead of giving them the blessing to launch immediately, the church leaders urged them to wait. "Take six months. Get some counseling. You just came through the extremely busy season of Michelle's residency. Make sure your marriage is strong before stepping into something this big."

The delay was another painful lesson in patience. Their church, despite being their home congregation, didn't actually know them well. Though Michelle and Adam had spent years leading a ministry for medical residents, that small group functioned mostly outside the church's core community. They had connections but not deep roots within the congregation.

This realization stung. They had always assumed their calling and passion were enough. But the church saw what they couldn't. They had spent so much time focused on getting *to* the field that they hadn't fully addressed how they would *stay* there. The stress of preparation had taken a toll, and their relationship, once filled with excitement and unity, had begun to show cracks.

Counseling wasn't something they had planned on, but it became a turning point. Michelle and Adam had to face a truth they hadn't fully acknowledged. The fact that they loved each other didn't mean they knew how to *work together*. They had always simply done the next thing on the checklist toward commissioning.

The counseling sessions forced them to pause and really see each other beyond the stress and logistics. They learned how to communicate in ways that weren't just about solving problems but about understanding each other's fears and motivations.

Michelle viewed the world like the determined athlete she had always been. Throughout her youth, she had spent four to five hours a day swimming alongside Olympic athletes to beat her personal records, win her heats, and score points for her swim team. She used that same passion, momentum, and regimented training to achieve all the goals in her life. She was convinced that sheer willpower could solve anything.

Adam was the opposite. He was steady and methodical. He needed time to process and plan before making a move. It wasn't that one of them was right and the other was wrong. They just approached the world in completely different ways. Their counselor helped them see that their strengths could complement rather than compete. They learned to listen, compromise, and trust that they were on the same team.

In the end, their church leaders were right. They recognized that residency is a terrible time for someone's spiritual, mental, physical, and relational health. Michelle was able to see that she had been in survival mode for years while she studied to become a family medicine physician. With the forced pause, she was able to see that she had never given their relationship time to thrive outside of a pressure-filled environment. Rushing overseas would have preyed on that weakness.

It was humbling. Adam and Michelle stopped pushing so hard and stopped trying to force open doors that weren't meant to open yet. Instead, they leaned into prayer, wise counsel, and the uncomfortable truth that God's timing didn't always match their own.

The months of waiting were difficult, but they were also refining. Their marriage became stronger as they learned to face struggles together. They started to really listen to each other and figure out how to give grace when stress made tempers short. They stopped focusing on how to get to the mission field and started focusing on how to be the kind of couple that thrived once they got there.

By the time their church finally gave them the green light, they weren't just eager missionaries with a dream. They were deeply aware of their need for God's guidance. As they prepared to leave, they did so with a newfound confidence—not in themselves but in the One who had called them.

BUILDING A HOME TOGETHER . . . LITERALLY

Michelle and Adam never planned to go overseas alone. From the beginning, they envisioned themselves as part of a team, a unit of like-minded, passionate medical professionals who could support one another through the challenges of mission work.

Their closest friends from their residency small group were another young couple—a fellow physician and an architect—who shared their vision. The four of them spent months praying, planning, and preparing together. As they all began contacting mission sites, they explained that they were a package deal.

With hearts settled on Ethiopia, the four of them made their first vision trip to meet with leaders at Soddo Christian Hospital, a well-established medical center in the southern part of the country.

Unfortunately, the hospital board declined their service. "We don't really need family doctors," they explained. "Our focus is surgery. You'd be better suited at the Mossy Foot Project in town."

This was not the answer or suggestion they had expected. The Mossy Foot Project was a nonprofit organization that focused on treating a painful disease characterized by swelling and rough, thickened skin on the feet caused by walking barefoot on certain types of soil. Though the project was an important public health initiative, it wasn't the medical mission they had envisioned.

They were trained to work in a hospital that provided full-spectrum care. They wanted to serve where they could treat the sick and train the next generation of Ethiopian physicians.

For weeks, the two couples wrestled with the rejection. *Had they misheard God? Were they supposed to change direction?* But their collective calling remained unchanged. Instead of receiving the rejection as a no, they decided to look at it as a challenge they were meant to engage in.

So they did.

They kept showing up, kept meeting with hospital leaders, and kept making their case. Slowly, minds began to change. The hospital board began to see the value in adding family medicine and public health to their services. They saw the need for Michelle's family medicine experience and the infrastructure support Adam could provide.

Finally, the organization changed its answer. "You can come," they told the two couples, "but we don't have housing for you. If you really want to be here, you'll have to build your own homes."

Building a house in Ethiopia as newly minted missionaries wasn't exactly what they had imagined. They had barely begun to raise their regular monthly support, let alone add on construction costs. But there was no alternative. If they wanted to join this medical community, they would need a place to live.

Adam the engineer and their teammate the architect immediately got to work designing and building their homes. As they sourced materials, sketched out plans with contractors, and found local builders, they became acquainted with the community in ways they hadn't expected.

Meanwhile, Michelle and her friend both threw themselves into fundraising, explaining to supporters why housing wasn't just a comfort but rather a necessity.

Money didn't pour in overnight. Sometimes the financial burden felt overwhelming, and they questioned whether they could actually pull it off. But God provided in ways they never expected. A friend of a friend made a donation. Brick by brick, the houses came together, and slowly they etched out their place in the community. The hospital staff, once unsure about their group, now began to see their dedication.

By the time Adam and Michelle's home was finished, it was more than just a building. It was a symbol of their commitment to Ethiopia, to their calling, and to each other. They hadn't taken the easy path, but they had met the challenge. And as they settled into life in Soddo, they knew this was exactly where they were meant to be.

WE'RE ALL IN THIS TOGETHER

Life in Ethiopia took on a rhythm. Michelle became the head of the pediatrics department at the hospital and oversaw public health outreach programs. Adam's engineering came in handy maintaining the facility. His willingness to jump into any type of problem meant he was quickly lending his skills to hospital building projects, infrastructure improvements, and information systems overhauls.

They settled into their work, juggling the intensity of medical missions with the unique challenges of a developing country. It wasn't easy. Supplies ran out, power outages disrupted surgeries, and the weight of community suffering was relentless. As part of the team of dedicated missionaries at the hospital, Michelle and Adam learned to navigate the hardships of life and work in Ethiopia.

In that time, their family grew as well. With children came the difficulty of balancing mission work with the daily demands of raising a family. Somehow, Michelle and Adam found ways to keep their marriage and children grounded by creating boundaries. They made a habit of sitting down for meals together, no matter how chaotic the day had been. Even when everything around them felt unpredictable, they always had each other.

A couple of years into their mission, Michelle and Adam were living out exactly what they had planned to do. But no amount of careful planning could prepare them for the chaos that hit in 2016. Political unrest rippled through Ethiopia, shaking the country with protests, roadblocks, and uncertainty. As foreigners, Adam and Michelle weren't direct targets, but the instability seeped into every part of their lives. It became harder to get supplies, and it was dangerous to travel between cities.

And then, in the midst of the chaos, two families abruptly decided to leave the mission. They weren't just colleagues;

they were people Michelle and Adam had trusted, prayed with, planned with, and leaned on during the hardest moments of their work at the hospital.

Though there was never just one reason for a departure, the challenges of living in a state of emergency were certainly extra pressure that brought it all to a head. Michelle and Adam acknowledged the difficult circumstances and knew that the families had chosen to exit Ethiopia by seeking God's plan for their lives. However, the lack of closure still cut deeply.

One day those workers were there, and the next they were gone. Those decisions blindsided Michelle and Adam, leaving them holding responsibilities they hadn't prepared for. There was no transition and no handoff. There was just a sudden void.

And with that void came a deep wound in Michelle's heart. She found that sense of woundedness growing into anger in ways she hadn't expected.

Weren't they all in this together?

Didn't those people know if they left, it would be more work for those who stayed?

Did anyone else on the team feel the same way?

How could she trust anyone on the team in the future?

How could she trust God to protect her from this kind of hurt when she was just obediently doing what He had called her to do?

The extra workload and the unanswered questions were hard enough, but there was also a new sense of disunity among the team. They had always gotten through hardships by knowing that other people on the field alongside them were persevering too. With two families leaving, the belief that "we're all in this together" suddenly came apart at the seams.

FORGIVENESS SOUNDS FINE IN THEORY

After facing these big losses and walking through the challenges of the national state of emergency, Michelle and Adam knew they needed a break before they burned out. Returning to America for a six-week sabbatical wasn't an easy choice. They had to step away from the work they had fought so hard to establish. But deep down, they knew they needed it. They needed space to breathe, process, and find a way forward that wasn't fueled by bitterness.

They found themselves back in the familiar office of their marriage counselor—the same one who had helped them prepare for life in Ethiopia. This time the struggle wasn't about communication in marriage. It was about healing wounds they weren't sure could be healed.

At first, they tried to keep the conversation logical. They explained what had happened when their teammates left. They described the weight of loss they were feeling. The counselor listened patiently, nodding in understanding, and then asked what exactly they wanted to happen.

The question caught them both off guard. What *did* they want to happen?

To see justice served? To receive an apology? To feel validated in their frustration?

The truth was, they didn't know. What they did know was that the bitterness was exhausting, and the anger wasn't making anything better.

The counselor gently reminded them that reconciliation wasn't always about resolution. It wasn't about getting the other person to admit their wrongs or even about restoring the relationship to what it once was. It was about their own hearts—about their willingness to surrender even their justified anger to God.

The counselor brought them into a space of grieving the losses and releasing them to God and shepherded them to see that the recent losses felt so hard because of deeply held pains from hard losses in their early lives. They were challenged to answer these questions:

Where was Jesus while they were in chaos?

Was He there?

Did they believe He was still holding them in His arms even when they felt so much uncertainty and loss?

They knew their counselor was right. They realized that their part was to seek peace with their partners by accepting where they might have failed and hurt them too. Their part was to apologize for their own failings and remember that Jesus was and still is in all of it.

The counseling was restorative, and Michelle and Adam returned to the field with intention and purpose. They knew what they needed to do, but doing it was another story.

CHOOSING RECONCILIATION

Back in Soddo, healing for Adam and Michelle didn't come overnight. The team had shrunk to its smallest number, and there were no kids for Adam and Michelle's children to be friends with. There were new challenges of loneliness and hard work. Their return to the field became marked by sadness and weariness.

In the next season, their team started to grow again, but Adam and Michelle found it harder to open their hearts to new people. After experiencing loss and loneliness, any team conflict created new hurts that reopened old ones. They found themselves lost in a cycle of being open enough to let people in and then being hurt enough to settle back into anger and bitterness.

Both Adam and Michelle wanted to move on and focus on who was there now, not on who had left. But it was hard to reconcile the desire to forgive when the emotions ran so deep.

One night, unable to sleep, Michelle lay there staring at the ceiling when she sensed God asking her a question: *Who do you want to be? Do you want to be a wounded person filled with anger and bitterness or someone who understands the fullness of the gospel and forgiveness and extends that to others?*

In the stillness, God's directive was clear: *Surrender. Lay it down. Let Me carry it.*

Tears welled up in Michelle's eyes as she realized how tightly she had been clinging to her anger and how much it had consumed her. In the end, it wasn't about justifying the hurt or making things right on her terms. It was about trust.

It had *always* been about trusting God every step of the way—in her refusal to date, in Adam's informal proposal three weeks into their dating relationship, in their rejections and delays, in the forced marriage counseling, in their home construction, and in all their work in Ethiopia. It had *all* been about trusting God.

And this moment? It was about trusting God to do the heart work of reconciliation. Michelle was finally able to surrender the hurt at His feet. She was tired of being bitter, suspicious, and distant. She wanted to be free, walking in the garden with Jesus and eager to share her life with those who were walking beside her.

In the weeks that followed, something slowly shifted. There was no quick, simple solution. Michelle and Adam didn't force friendships that had run their course or magically make everyone agree. Instead, they simply surrendered to God and chose reconciliation. They refused to let bitterness set up permanent residence in their hearts. They woke up each day and chose grace, even when it felt unnatural and when holding a grudge seemed far more satisfying.

Conversations that had once felt impossible started happening. They slowly rebuilt bridges that had seemed burned. Even in the tension, they saw glimpses of redemption. Their ministry in Ethiopia deepened, no longer weighed down by bitterness. Their marriage, once tested by conflict, grew stronger through the shared experience of surrendering their hurts to God. Even their children saw the difference as they watched their parents choose grace over anger.

It wasn't about fixing anything. It was about believing that God was always in the business of healing what they never could. Reconciliation became more than just a one-time act. It became a way of life, a choice they would have to make again and again— not because it was easy but because it was worth it.

And though nothing was perfect, Michelle and Adam knew one thing for certain: God had brought them to Ethiopia not just to serve but to be transformed.

MY TAKE: THE GIFT OF SURRENDER

I'm always struck by how often God asks us to lay something down before He gives us something greater. Adam had a clear plan: career, stability, and family. But then came that dream about Michelle and the motorcycle. It was a relational nudge, but it was also a calling to surrender, and that kind of surrender flies in the face of everything our culture tells us to pursue.

The truth is that God will often let us walk the path we choose. We can still follow Christ without fully surrendering, but I know from my own life that we won't live as fully or fruitfully as we could. I, too, have had to release my carefully built plans and say, "Okay, Lord, have Your way." It's rarely easy, and frankly, it's often scary. Most of us want God's best but on *our* timeline and in *our* way. What I've learned and what I see in the Yateses' story is that when we truly surrender, we begin to operate on the strength of the Holy Spirit rather than our own, and that changes everything.

From the beginning, Michelle and Adam were called on to surrender their plans. They experienced rejection, delay, and disappointment on their way to the field. They hit resistance and wisely and eventually slowed down.

I want readers, especially those preparing to go overseas, to hear this clearly: When you face resistance, don't just push through it. Ask what God might be saying. Many who rush forward too quickly carry unresolved brokenness into places where the stakes are incredibly high. And that brokenness, if left unaddressed, doesn't stay small; it becomes magnified.

That is why I'm so grateful that Michelle and Adam were willing to share their story. They could have kept quiet about the counseling, the cracks, the bitterness, and the forgiveness. But their honesty is a gift. It reflects what the MedSend Longevity Project is all about—helping missionaries pause, get help, and do the inner work necessary to be healthy and whole because unresolved hurt doesn't just affect you. It impacts your spouse, your teammates, and the people you're trying to serve. *If it's broken, go get help.*

I was struck by Michelle's moment of surrender. Lying in bed that night, she could have chosen to hold onto bitterness. Instead, she chose to trust, to let God do the fixing. She opened her hands, let go of her right to be angry or feel justified, and chose the harder, better path.

So wherever you are—whether you're preparing to go abroad, are already serving, or are simply trying to walk faithfully in your everyday life—ask yourself: *Where is God asking me to surrender? What bitterness am I carrying that's limiting what God can do through me?*

The answer might just be the beginning of something far greater than you imagined.

CHAPTER 11

RELATIONSHIPS ARE THE MISSION

ERIC AND RACHEL MCLAUGHLIN

E ric McLaughlin knocked on the front door of his neighbor's house. His question was simple, but the implications were heavy: *Should they still meet as a group for prayer and fellowship?*

That might seem an unusual question to ask in a missionary community. Under normal circumstances, the answer would be *of course* or *why not?* But these were not normal days. The McLaughlins and their teammates were in the middle of the biggest conflict they'd experienced while on mission in Burundi: COVID-19.

The door opened, and Eric stepped back, trying out the new "social distancing" thing. His question was met with a firm vote to put all meetings on hold. The response was passionate, emphasizing the risks of gathering during a global pandemic, especially for doctors with patients who were relying on them.

Eric moved on to the next home, wondering if others would feel the same. Before he could even knock, the door swung open, and someone greeted him warmly—no distancing needed. This time, his inquiry was met with enthusiasm. These teammates, weary of isolation, were eager for fellowship and readily agreed to join the prayer gathering.

It was clear that it was not going to be easy to find an option that everyone felt good about.

Eric continued down the dirt road to the third house. The response there was more cautious and undecided. Those friends were concerned about both the health risks and the importance of community. They preferred to go along with whatever the majority decided, leaving the final outcome uncertain.

Eric nodded and said he'd be back later with more news. He went along his way, making sure each member of their tight-knit community contributed their wishes, concerns, and opinions. Yes, it took time and emotional investment, but after living in community the past seven years in Burundi, he knew this approach was vital.

In fact, it was this approach—this calling to the community—that had sustained Eric and Rachel's ministry all these years.

COWORKERS VS. COMMUNITY

It all began in high school when Rachel sensed she was called to medical missions. She stayed true to this desire and eventually entered medical school in California. In her third year, she attended the Global Missions Health Conference (GMHC) in Louisville, Kentucky, where she met Eric, a second-year med student at the University of Michigan.

A mutual friend had told Eric to seek out and befriend Rachel. After all, they were both Christians, and both were studying medicine. As their mutual friend had predicted, they hit it off right away when they connected at the conference, and a long-distance friendship began.

Over the next year, their friendship grew into a romantic relationship. Eventually, Rachel chose Michigan for several fourth-year rotations in order to be near Eric. They both finished their residencies. She studied to be an ob-gyn, and Eric entered family medicine.

Together, they dreamed big.

Rachel shared her desire to serve people internationally as a missionary. Though Eric had not committed to missions, he had a strong calling to make a difference in people's lives as a family doctor. And more importantly, he knew that no matter where they ended up or what they did, he was meant to face the world alongside Rachel.

Rachel felt called to medical missions; Eric felt called to Rachel.

Feeling this sentiment deep in his heart, he asked her to marry him, knowing that meant he would be going overseas.

Their international journey had a rough start. On a month-long overseas rotation, Eric and Rachel had their first taste of the kind of difficulties that can arise on a missionary team. They observed doctors who functioned more like coworkers than a true community, which created tension and isolation.

Some doctors were intensely committed, pulling all-nighters and pushing themselves to the limit. Others took a more measured approach, focusing on sustainability and setting boundaries.

That led to frustration on both sides. The high-intensity doctors felt like others weren't pulling their weight, while the more reserved doctors felt overshadowed and pressured to match an unsustainable pace.

Rachel and Eric came away from that experience with a conviction about intentional community-building. Instead of defaulting to a "you do your thing, and I'll do mine" mindset, they had a sense that building strong relationships needed to be part of the mission itself. Without that strong foundation, conflicts seemed harder to resolve, and there was a feeling of disunity.

Eric and Rachel coupled that experience with data from the Reducing Missionary Attrition Project (ReMAP), which found that interpersonal conflict was a leading cause of missionaries leaving the field.[1] After their short-term rotation experience, they could see how that statistic could be true and found themselves asking how intentional community-building would make a difference. What mattered most for a successful mission?

Together they landed on three things:

- A calling to relationship with colleagues.
- A perspective that relationships are part of the mission.
- A team committed to being the Body of Christ.

They believed that in order to sustain a missions lifestyle in the future, they would have to intentionally build that community from the ground up.

GATHER THE TEAM

Returning from that overseas trip, Rachel and Eric knew they wanted to serve with people they knew and trusted. From the beginning, they saw missions as a way of life that would shape their family, their friendships, and their faith.

They didn't want to be in a situation where they were constantly at odds with their colleagues or struggling to find emotional and spiritual support. Instead, they dreamed of doing the work alongside like-minded people—friends who could share the load, encourage each other in hard times, and create a community that felt like family. They wanted a team that was a true support system—real friendships with people they could trust in every aspect of life.

That desire became reality when they got an email from two other families who shared the same vision. The Cropseys were already long-term friends with Rachel and Eric, and the Faders were all in on joining them too. These couples had been independently discussing the same issues and were looking to build a team that would be a community.

The timing couldn't have been more perfect. Rachel and Eric immediately saw the value of going overseas with a group of people they already respected and enjoyed rather than taking a leap into the unknown. So in 2007, the three families made the commitment to go wherever God led them, and they would go together.

Their first stop was Tenwek Hospital in Kenya where they agreed to spend two years as a trial period. They knew that when they arrived in Kenya they weren't testing out a location so much as each other. They had all committed to pursue long-term missions as a team, but they knew that good intentions weren't enough. Living and working together in high-stress environments would stretch their patience, reveal their weaknesses, and force them to navigate conflict in real time.

It was a little like marriage—exciting, full of potential, but also requiring deep commitment and compromise. They all approached those two years with a mix of hope and nervous anticipation, knowing that if their friendships and working relationships couldn't survive this trial run, they wouldn't survive years on the field together.

As they served at Tenwek, they also traveled across Africa searching for the right place to plant long-term roots. It was a daunting task.

Madagascar held incredible medical opportunities, a clear need, and the potential for meaningful work. Burundi, on the other hand, was one of the most medically underserved places in the world.

Both locations were appealing for different reasons, but the more the families talked and prayed, the more they realized that their decision was more about each other than geography. They weren't simply looking for the best mission hospital or the most strategic location. What mattered most to them was a place that best matched the unique calling and gifts of the team. The realization hit them slowly but undeniably. They were more certain about their calling to *each other* than about any particular destination.

When they finally chose Burundi, it wasn't because it was the easiest option. In fact, it was probably the hardest. The country had limited infrastructure, few resources, and an overwhelming need. But that was exactly why they felt they could make a difference there together.

They knew that one family alone might not survive the pressures of working in such an intense environment, but as a team, they could carry the weight together. They could push through burnout, support each other's families, and create a sense of home in a place where the challenges might otherwise drive them away. In the end, Burundi was where they were called to build a community.

THE TEAM COMMITMENT

When Eric and Rachel first arrived in Burundi in 2013, their group was small and built on friendship, trust, and shared experiences. They knew why they were there, and they shared the same vision for a community of medical missionaries.

But as more families joined, they realized that unspoken expectations weren't enough to build that same level of buy-in. New people required more intentional vision-casting.

The original families suggested creating a team commitment statement that would lay out their vision and some core values they all agreed to live by. That wasn't a new concept. They were simply putting onto paper what they had already been doing, but this way it would be clear to everyone. They drew from the idea that churches all over the world made covenants with their members. Though they weren't a church plant, they were definitely in Burundi together to serve as the Body of Christ.

No one wanted to dictate every aspect of life. They simply wanted something in writing to ensure that they and anyone joining the community were on the same page. With the old church dictum in mind—in essentials unity, in nonessentials liberty, and in all things charity—they drafted a short document that outlined the mission, vision, and values of their team.

It wasn't about rules or logistics; it was about principles and how they treated each other. It outlined how they would handle conflict and how they prioritized relationships as part of the mission itself.

- Relationships aren't just important; they're part of the mission.
- Everyone will give their best but will also take time off to recharge.

- People will live differently, and that's okay as long as it doesn't divide the team.

- Disagreements will happen, but we will work through them with honesty and grace.

- Worship, prayer, and team gatherings will keep us grounded and unified.

- We will choose to see the best in each other and speak with kindness, even when things get tough.

Over time, that team commitment evolved. Every few years, the group revised it to make sure it still reflected the heart of their community and forged strong relationships within the team. It's been an anchor for new members of the team and has helped people discern whether this is the right place for them before they uproot their lives in the United States.

For Rachel, Eric, and the others, this document is a reflection of who they are and why they choose to do this work together.

A DAY IN THE LIFE

Rachel sighed as she stepped out of the hospital and into the cool Burundi evening. It had been one of those days, the kind where everything felt just a little heavier than usual—a complicated C-section, a baby with breathing complications, and a young mother who might not survive the night. Some days, the weight of it all pressed down so hard that Rachel wasn't sure she could keep going.

But as she walked the familiar path back home, she heard the sound of laughter—loud, joyful, unburdened. The team's kids were playing outside, chasing each other through the red dirt, their giggles carrying through the compound. For a moment, she just stopped and watched. That was why they had come together as a team. Through all of it, they had built a life worth staying for.

When Rachel reached home, she checked her phone and saw a notification from the shared Google calendar. Someone had signed out the van for a grocery run the next day. That meant she and Eric would have to shift plans and take the little car instead—not ideal for the bumpy road into town.

Sharing vehicles was just part of life there. They had four cars for ten families, and it required a constant dance of scheduling, flexibility, and sometimes just handing over the keys and figuring it out later. She remembered how strange it had felt when they first started this. Back in the United States, she and Eric had always had their own cars and their own space. But here, life was shared in every way possible, down to who got to drive where on any given day. And somehow, it worked.

Of course, living in such a close community wasn't always easy. Raising kids together meant that different parenting styles clashed. One family let their kids roam free while another was more cautious. Inevitably, frustrations would rise. Living as a team meant learning how to navigate situations where their lives overlapped much more than they would have in the States.

School held its own delicate balance. Missionary moms were teaching each other's kids, trying to keep friendships intact while also handing out grades and discipline. Conflict was a certainty, but the difference was that everyone had committed to working through it. In Burundi, there was no disappearing into separate lives or finding a new social circle at the end of the day. These people were it. These were the people they did life with, and that meant facing the hard conversations instead of avoiding them.

Later that evening, the team gathered for worship. Sitting around a campfire under the brilliant Burundi stars, kids curling up in laps, and everyone singing songs together, Rachel looked around and felt an overwhelming sense of gratitude. As a fairly individualistic, happy-to-be-introverted person, it was one of the biggest surprises of her life that she had ended up in a community like this.

The struggles were real—the exhaustion, the disagreements, the endless logistic hurdles of living as foreigners in a place where power outages and water shortages were just part of the rhythm of life. But they didn't do this alone. They carried each other.

When someone had a bad day, there was always a meal waiting at their door. When a kid was sick, another parent stepped in to help. When grief or doubt crept in, there was always someone to sit and pray with. Even during the stressful and confusing days of COVID-19, the team persisted in supporting one another. They listened, worked through differences of opinion, and adjusted.

God had called them to this life with all its challenges and beauty. And He had called them to one another. Through every shared burden and every shared joy, God was building something far greater than any of them could have done alone. As they honored God by honoring each other, their community was creating a beautiful picture of God's coming Kingdom.

Their relationships continue to be more than a means to an end. Their relationships *are* the mission.

MY TAKE: KNOWN BY OUR LOVE

Independence is the American way. Even missionaries with genuine hearts to serve God and others often struggle to break free from an individualistic Western mindset. We Americans are inherently programmed to think, "I have a calling. I have prepared myself. This is my mission, and I'm going to protect my family while fulfilling it."

We are willing to sacrifice personally—selling houses, cars, and possessions—and are eager to commit wholeheartedly to our individual vision of ministry. Yet ironically, this very mindset can create division and isolation in missionary teams.

Eric and Rachel's story is a compelling contrast to this norm. The way they have intentionally built a unified, relationally driven community is incredibly unique and special. From the beginning, they entered overseas ministry more committed to their team than to specific individual ministry goals.

The irony here is profound. Many missionaries serve in community-based cultures that inherently value interconnectedness and mutual dependence. American missionaries often arrive armed with an independent, results-driven mindset. I probably don't have to explain how that can cause tension both in the community and among missionary coworkers. Sadly, my observations line up with the statistics. The primary reason missionaries leave the field prematurely isn't external hardship or persecution; it is relational conflicts within their teams.

The intentional pursuit of relationships above personal agendas (even godly ones) is what makes Eric, Rachel, and their team so distinct. Their calling was as much to each other as it was to the work. And that meant they had to do things differently. They had to listen to each other deeply. They had to collaborate. Even as they developed a team commitment, they compromised to come together on a document they could all embrace. Their approach beautifully illustrates the fundamental biblical truth that we Christ-followers will be known by our love.

In a setting where the needs are overwhelming and the temptation to focus solely on medical outcomes could quickly become the main focus, the McLaughlins' dedication to relationships as the primary mission is remarkable. All of it matters to God—physical healing, spiritual awakening, and love for one another.

CHAPTER 12

HOW TO FINISH WELL

CHRISTINA AND GREG MILLER

After eight years in Malawi, Christina and Greg Miller were finally back in the United States. They were jet-lagged and sick, but that's not what made this plane trip memorable.

What made it memorable was that they landed in California the same day the devastating wildfires began in Los Angeles in January 2025.

As they sat on the tarmac after their plane landed, they watched text messages light up their phones. *Did you land yet? Are you near the fire? Is your house okay?*

They had bought their house just five months earlier. It was a charming, California-priced house that had been furnished by generous family members and Craigslist finds. They'd barely spent more than three weeks in it during trips back and forth from Malawi. And now, after giving away nearly everything they owned in Malawi, they were coming home to a place they'd hardly lived in, wondering if it was even still standing.

Arriving during a natural disaster was a lot to process. As it was, they already struggled with feeling suspended between worlds. Though they had plenty of little problems that had piled up over the last few months (expired visas and a terminated house lease), they weren't ending their mission and returning to California because of failure or burnout.

In fact, things had been going really well. Greg's work with churches in the central region had been thriving. Christina's clinic-based efforts and public health initiatives were transforming communities, especially through the local pastors they trained as health champions. Even after they left, they knew their projects would keep growing.

There was no disaster, moral failure, or breaking point. They had simply and consistently asked themselves, *Are we still helping? Or are we now in the way?*

That question followed them through customs, through the Los Angeles fires, and through the front door of a house they'd never really settled into. (Yes, it was still standing somehow.)

They had just given the last eight years to building something in Malawi. They were still in love with the work and still in relationship with many of the people. But for the first time in their ministry life, they weren't asking, *How do we stay?* Instead, they asked, *What does it mean to leave well?*

A BALANCE OF HEAD AND HEART

Christina and Greg had met years earlier when they were fellow athletes on their college track team in California. They would lace up their shoes and occasionally run alongside each other, but more often they tried to outsprint each other.

Christina was energetic, focused, and structured, and had already made up her mind that she'd be heading to the mission field—as a single person if necessary. In fact, she used to tell people, only half-jokingly, that "a man is the number-one reason a woman doesn't make it to the mission field." She certainly wasn't at school to get her Mrs. degree. To her, marriage was more of a risk than a goal.

Though Greg was attracted to her, he got it. He was friendly, but he had his own goals in mind. His dream was to pursue a graduate degree at seminary.

After college, they went their separate ways. Christina stayed in California to attend medical school and complete a double residency in family and preventative medicine. Greg left for graduate school.

While they were both in school, Greg and Christina reconnected and started dating, but Christina was still concerned about a relationship getting in the way of her calling.

That changed almost two years later when Christina completed a medical rotation in Papua, New Guinea. The doctor she shadowed was everything Christina admired—an intense woman who could handle C-sections, manage complex cases, and power through long hours. She was the overachiever's overachiever. In other words, she was Christina's kind of person.

But the reality was that the doctor didn't do her job alone. Her husband, a pastor, was serving right alongside her. He taught at the local pastoral training center while she practiced at the hospital. Their partnership worked really well, and suddenly,

Christina had a real-life example of how marriage didn't need to be a threat to her mission. In fact, it was possible that marriage could actually enhance her impact.

She had gone to Papua, New Guinea, thinking she might never marry, but she returned to the States hoping that Greg would propose soon. She realized what Greg had known for a while, that despite having opposite personalities, their callings were actually compatible.

Christina wanted to work where medicine could impact entire populations. She loved systems, organization, and long-term goals. She thrived on structure and plans. Greg was wired for support, and theology gave him a common language to use. His pastoral instincts to listen, tell stories, and draw connections made him come alive.

They quickly realized that they were using different tools from the same toolbox, and that box could definitely be used for the same purpose.

Unlike a lot of the stories in this book where couples and their children head to the mission field, Greg and Christina agreed early in their relationship that children would not be part of their story. They had a deep conviction that their God-given talents were meant to be channeled with undivided focus. They would pour everything into their mission, and not even a natural pull toward parenthood would divert them from that calling.

Their mutual desire for ministry impact and the unique balance of head and heart reflected in their relationship would eventually take them to Malawi. After looking at every location in their mission network, they found one spot where both of them could do the work they were actually built for.

In Malawi, Christina could see patients and offer community-based public health. Greg could teach theology and equip local pastors. It was the perfect location for them to serve together.

NOT THERE JUST TO FILL IN

Christina and Greg landed in Malawi with a shared sense of calling and an eagerness to begin their respective jobs. At first, they did what most first-term missionaries do. They tried to fit in and survive.

Christina jumped into clinical work at a mission hospital while Greg taught theology at the Nazarene college nearby. They shared a house with spotty power and overly confident geckos. They made friends, and they made mistakes. They learned how to filter water and haggle for vegetables at the market. They slowly started to understand the rhythms of life in the heart of Africa.

But as time went on, they began to see why missionaries struggled in this country.

Christina worked in hospitals that treated symptoms well but seemed disinterested in causes. She'd see the same preventable conditions over and over again—hypertension, malnutrition, and infections—that could have been avoided with basic education or clean water. Every time she tried to push upstream by talking about prevention or systemic change, she hit a wall. What motivated many in the medical community were profit incentives. It was a subtle message: Stay in your lane, treat your patients, and stop hoping for systems to change.

Meanwhile, Greg started seeing how deeply that same logic crept into church life. Missionaries ran the programs, but the locals carried out instructions only as long as outside inputs lasted. Despite his passion for teaching, Greg realized that he was slowly being asked to do less teaching and more filling in. He was asked to show up for classes at the college because he was the foreigner who looked the part.

After a few years of this, Greg and Christina finally realized what they were really there to do. Christina scaled back her clinical hours and began working directly with local leaders such as pastors and community health workers to equip them to lead preventative health efforts from the ground up.

Greg leaned all the way into his work with more than 120 Nazarene churches in the region. He preached only when asked to and instead focused on teaching the Bible. He trained pastors to teach doctrine through sermons and also be shepherds of the people.

Together, the Millers found their groove. They held workshops on everything from women's health and childhood diseases to mental health and food sustainability. Most of all, they mentored local leaders and intentionally stepped back when those leaders stepped forward. Greg and Christina found that the pastors were the hands and feet of Jesus, so they continued to equip them in health education and mentor them in discipleship.

The impact and growth were real. Communities where they trained new pastors suddenly held Bible studies and small-scale health initiatives. Women who'd never spoken in public now taught others about nutrition.

Their collective vision created a strong alignment in their marriage. They couldn't solve every problem that came up, but the work felt much lighter when they carried the weight of it together. They learned in that season to celebrate the success of someone else rising up to lead. They knew that if they couldn't see the value in that, they were missing the point entirely.

A SUSTAINABLE MISSION

Over the years, Christina and Greg's work stretched beyond the hospital clinics and the classrooms. They were building systems and training leaders to address the challenges. And eventually they discovered that one of the biggest challenges in Malawi was farming.

Subsistence agriculture was survival. People grew just enough food to live and not a handful more. Nongovernmental organizations (NGOs) came in with training and techniques, promising better yields. Some offered seeds and equipment, but hardly any communities tried the new methods because the risk was enormous.

If they failed, the people would lose their food and their income. And if they worked, a good harvest could invite jealousy and theft. In communities where scarcity shaped the culture, success came with suspicion.

Greg and Christina saw this tension play out again and again until one day someone asked, "What if, instead of an outsider or NGO introducing new farming methods, it was the local church? What if pastors led the way?" Local pastors who held the people's trust and had deep roots in the community had much more potential for bringing sustainable hope and healing than specialized outsiders.

A handful of church leaders agreed to test this theory with the Millers. They separated a small piece of land into a demonstration plot. Then they organized a women's group and a men's group that both had a say in what would happen and an understanding of what was at stake in the harvest. They were willing to try it for one season on just this one field.

That year, something remarkable happened. The yield tripled. Rows of maize, taller and fuller than anyone expected, became a miracle crop. The abundance became a new lifeline for the community as widows and families who'd been one meal away from desperation had more than enough to eat. They shared the surplus and celebrated.

For the first time in a long time, the people were able to imagine a future where they weren't just trying to survive. Suddenly, every family and farmer wanted to try the new technique. They were willing because their own people vouched for the method.

Greg and Christina saw firsthand how training up local leaders and utilizing the church as the vehicle for change worked. They realized that with this strategy, anything was possible. Their mission shifted from doing the work themselves to walking alongside the people who were already there, already showing up, and already trying and leading.

The philosophy led them to seek out more local leaders, people who were already serving the community or going the extra mile. Greg looked for seminarians who liked to teach after hours or were willing to lead without a title. Christina took note of the health workers who visited the sick without being asked and who offered to share tools with whoever needed them.

The Millers broke down the Western perspective that people needed to reach a certain level of professionalism before they were worthy of investment. Instead, they sought out leaders who were already there planting fields, teaching neighbors, praying with patients, or running the clinics.

They began to sow a new legacy in Malawi: missionaries who create sustainable, long-term impact.

WHEN THE WORK IS DONE

Greg and Christina's work was thriving. The pastors they trained were leading health workshops on their own. Community projects had momentum. One of Christina's former clinic directors had flown to Washington, DC, to present at a major public health conference. Their vision was coming to life.

That is exactly why they began to wonder if it was time to go.

It started with a question: *Are we still helping?* Was their presence becoming a crutch? Were they creating a funnel for real growth?

Greg began to feel it in the classroom. He was being asked to teach classes labeled "English-medium." The leaders who put him in those classes depended on his heart to help the locals learn the gospel, but he knew it wasn't because he was the best for the role. It was because he *looked* the best for the role. He was simply filling teaching gaps since he was a white man with a doctorate on his resume.

Christina started noticing it in the clinics. When she trained doctors on something like chronic disease management, it didn't lead to more empowered care. It led to more referrals to her—the white doctor, the foreigner who "knew better" or at least could bring in more high-paying patients than other clinicians.

In their own opinion, they were no longer useful as missionaries if they were being pushed into the center of the ring as the main event. The roles they were filling seemed to undermine the sustainability of locally led systems, and that was the opposite of what they had gone to Malawi to do.

With a newfound conviction, they began to envision what it would look like to *finish well*. How could they step aside without stepping out? Was it possible to be available but not in the way? And ultimately they asked if God was calling them to leave while things were good.

For a long time they believed they needed to stay until the work was "done." It's a common conviction among missionaries. Many remain until circumstances force their departure rather than consciously thinking through when the work might be done. And when exactly is the work ever really "done"?

It was uncomfortable trying to explain to their colleagues that they believed it was a good time to leave when their ministries were in a good place. They felt a constant urge to defend themselves. And at the core of this tension came a question about identity. Did they still have a calling to missions if they were returning to live in a house in California, *not Africa*?

Turning to Scripture to find answers, Christina and Greg realized that they had never considered—nor had anyone had ever told them—that the Apostle Paul never stayed anywhere longer than three years. They just assumed that missions were supposed to follow the old-fashioned model where they stayed in one place for life. Using Paul's ministry as affirmation, they ultimately concluded that God was telling them that their chapter in Malawi was ending.

Unfortunately, the ending wasn't clean.

Small problems began to emerge one by one. First, their visas weren't renewed. Technically, this was normal because three renewals were often the limit. Their landlord also grew unhappy with how housesitters cared for the property while they were in the States on furlough. She kicked them out with a month's notice, and the missionary houses their organization owned in that city were not available. Suddenly, the Millers were without a home in Malawi, and the only one they had was half a world away in California. While no single circumstance was insurmountable, it did speed them toward what they already had seen on the horizon—the end of the time they could serve sustainably in Malawi.

With the clock ticking on the number of days they could spend in the country on their expired visas, they ended up saying their goodbyes in a flurry. They had just three weeks to pack up eight years of their lives. They flew back to California without another mission assignment lined up. All they had was the home they had recently bought in a neighborhood only a canyon away from the Los Angeles fires.

Though their future was uncertain and their departure abrupt, they were confident in the season's end. And they fully believed they weren't forced out. They were just faithful enough to leave when it was time.

DEFINING CALLING

Even though they're now across the world from Malawi at the time of this writing, the Millers remain deeply connected to the work they started there. Because their true goal was to build a sustainable, self-sufficient community, they see stepping away when they did as a sign of mission success.

Modern technology allows Christina to continue offering care from afar. She remains in close partnership with the clinic's director. Their collaboration extends beyond daily operations to coauthoring journal articles. Former trainees ask her to review programs or help craft policy, and she continues equipping pastors and nurses to reach their communities.

Greg would tell you that the pastors he trained are doing a better job than he ever could, and that brings him immense pride. He started consulting with mission groups about organizational health, transition plans, longevity, and burnout. With all he's learned on the mission field, he knows the value of building something that doesn't rely on your presence to survive.

Though they still don't know what's next, the Millers' calling hasn't ended. It turns out that a calling is a series of courageous entrances and humble exits in which you finish well. Greg calls it the long game. Christina just calls it life.

MY TAKE: PASSING THE BATON

What exactly is our role as Westerners in missions today? This is a conversation that's been evolving for decades, but it feels more urgent now than ever. I can appreciate the emotional weight of Greg and Christina's personal wrestling. *When do we step away so others can take over? What does it look like to finish well?*

Mission leaders are facing the same questions. Changing times and changing strategies mean the traditional Western mission model is shifting—because it has to.

One of the key dynamics driving that shift is the growth of the church and ministries in the Global South. These nations are not just mission fields anymore. They are becoming sending countries themselves. They are planting churches, raising evangelists, and building ministries. Westerners are still needed but not in the same ways they once were. In healthcare where the needs are staggering, there's an undeniable opening for healthcare professionals to go and serve with compassion in Christ's name, while also equipping and empowering national leaders.

But it's a delicate balance. In healthcare, you can't just drop in, teach a few lessons, and then expect people to run with them. It takes years to train skilled nurses, doctors, and healthcare educators. And it can take decades to understand what is going on below the surface in a culture in order to understand what people are really thinking and figure out how an intervention can truly become self-sustaining. Meanwhile, there are local pastors, evangelists, and church planters stepping into their God-given roles, and we have to be careful not to overshadow them. Sometimes just our presence as Westerners inadvertently places us in a position of authority we never intended to take, and that can unintentionally stifle what God is doing through national leaders.

And still, it would be naive to say that the Western missionary is no longer needed. There are still places in the world where people have yet to hear the name of Christ. God is still at work raising up workers from every corner of the world. The role of the Western missionary may be changing, but it's far from obsolete.

At MedSend, we're investing in the longevity of Western missionaries on the field while also pouring resources into scholarships to train nationals. I get to see firsthand what God is doing globally, and it's incredible. The handoff might be slow and sometimes awkward, but it's happening. And that's a good thing.

CHAPTER 13

BUILT TO LAST

OMEGA AND JULIE EDWARDS

E ight thousand eight hundred miles—that's the distance
between rural New Zealand and upstate New York. It's also
the distance between a quiet girl who rarely raised her voice
and a preacher's kid who grew up surrounded by many voices—
between Julie and Omega.

On paper, they were opposites.

Julie was the daughter of dairy farmers whose life was tied to
weather patterns and livestock feed. Her world was quiet. Church
was small, and faith was private though lived out. Her parents
weren't missionaries or pastors, just steady believers who taught

their kids that God could be trusted and obedience was enough. As a child, Julie imagined what faithfulness looked like, a type of calling that plants and waters without needing to see the harvest.

She learned early how to listen, be still, and work without complaining. She didn't call attention to herself but noticed everything around her, especially the needs of people in her community. When the opportunity came to serve at an orphanage in Mozambique, she said yes. The flashiness of missional commissioning was not enticing to her, but she knew that God was in the mission. As a young adult, she left her home quietly and ended up serving faithfully abroad for five years.

Omega's path was much louder. He was child number nine in a family of eleven in a house overflowing with love, faith, and ... well, noise. His father, a Baptist pastor from the deep South, moved the family north in hopes of escaping the lasting generational effects of segregation and racial violence. Despite his father's faithful conviction and worn-out Bible, Omega saw how a conservative Baptist family could be like fish out of water in the liberal Northeast.

By high school, Omega already knew his life wouldn't follow a straight line. He was drawn to medicine but driven by ministry. He wasn't yet sure how those two would fit together, but he knew one thing: He wanted to serve. And when a mission trip to Mozambique opened up, he said yes. It was a short-term opportunity to help at an orphanage. He didn't know it then, but he was walking straight into the rest of his life.

In the dust of Mozambique, Julie and Omega met—two people doing the same work in the same forgotten corner of the world.

He noticed her first—how she moved through the orphanage with a quiet presence. She wasn't loud or commanding, and she didn't offer advice unless asked. But when she spoke, he noticed that the kids listened. So did the other staff members.

Omega had seen a lot of moves by the Holy Spirit by then. He'd heard thousands of altar calls as a pastor's son, but he hadn't seen many people like Julie. Faith was woven into her very spirit. It caught him off guard—in a good way.

Their conversations were simple at first, mostly work updates and prayer requests. They occasionally shared a meal if their schedules overlapped. But even in those early days, they started to realize that their callings were being shaped together. They saw the world through the same faithful lens of mission work.

Omega had gone to Mozambique for a short-term assignment, and he didn't expect to find his future wife. But looking back, he says it like it was obvious: "This was the woman the Lord brought for me."

They were a boy from New York and a girl from New Zealand, separated by oceans and upbringing, futures converging in the middle of a dusty courtyard in Africa. Sometimes the easiest connections are those that God Himself makes. That connection would only grow from there—a relationship, marriage, kids, and a move to the United States so Omega could finish medical school.

A WHOLE-FAMILY MINISTRY

After medical school, Omega learned to navigate the rhythm of a doctor's office—phones constantly ringing, pens clicking and scribbling on clipboards, nurses swiftly walking down tight hallways, appointments piling up from morning to dusk. After years of training at some of the best intuitions in the country, he opened his own practice in California, practicing infectious disease and internal medicine. He was doing what he'd always wanted to do—helping people and supporting his family.

He knew he'd need to address the deep calling inside his heart one day, but it didn't happen immediately. His draw toward mission work had always intrigued him, but now he wasn't sure how to pursue it as a husband and father. For five years, he operated his own practice with Julie by his side raising their family.

As the years went by, the pressures of owning his own practice in the States started to pile up. He had to deal with the constant stress of potentially being sued, a downside to his career choice that he had not understood as a medical student.

Julie felt her calling stir in those five years as well. Between school drop-offs and meal prep, errands, and bedtime routines, she began to feel ready for a big move of God. She could feel herself being called, and the time to act with obedience was coming.

Mozambique had been the beginning for them, but this time they weren't single and in their early twenties with their entire futures ahead of them. Now they had a thriving medical practice, a home, and four children. They had many reasons to stay and say *no, not yet*.

But Omega and Julie had a history of saying yes.

As they prayed and waited for God's direction, they began to feel convicted to invite their children into the calling. It was not easy to bring their children into adult-sized decisions, but they realized that moving to a remote corner of the world would have whole-family consequences.

One day, while driving the kids to school, they asked, "Would you pray with us? Would you ask God what He might want for our family?"

The children were still in grade school, but the question didn't faze them. They were accustomed to praying as a family because Julie and Omega made a point of praying together regularly. When they asked their kids to listen to God's voice, it wasn't shocking. It made absolute sense to ask God what their next steps should be.

Days passed and questions floated. *What about our friends? What about school? What about all our things and our house?*

Beneath their childlike concerns, a deep faith was forming, and discernment began to grow.

After a few weeks, one of their daughters spoke with great assurance. "This is what we're meant to do as a family."

Julie and Omega knew in that instant that this wasn't just *their* calling. It was their family's calling.

The decision unraveled everything they knew. They sought out a global sending initiative and began the process to go abroad.

Omega began to let go of his practice. He had built it from the ground up, and selling it was no small feat. Years of his life had been spent within the walls of that clinic, and his colleagues respected him. But when God's invitation comes, it rarely fits inside what we've built. He is greater and goes beyond. So Omega let it go.

Their home and belongings were next. They packed what they could and gave away the rest. Moving internationally with four kids was chaotic. There was paperwork and passports. They tossed out baby clothes they had wanted to save as keepsakes but wouldn't fit in a box and weren't useful for the future. The entire process was excitement wrapped in a sentiment of sadness.

But through every box and every prayer, one thing remained clear: They weren't doing this alone. This was a family story, not just a sacrifice led by parents and endured by their children. Omega, Julie, Lizzie, Evelyn, Oliver, and Francie were on this journey together.

Next stop: Dar es Salaam, Tanzania.

CHOOSING HEALTH OVER HUSTLE

In the early days of their mission, it was tempting to do too much. The new culture, new language, new ministry, and new home all begged for urgency.

Only after five years of living, adjusting, and serving in a private local hospital did the next step become clear: It was time for the Edwardses to open their own medical clinic. It took eighteen months because establishing a new entity in the community was not a straightforward process.

Though they were fortunate to have a preexisting building with modern amenities, Omega faced a lot of regulatory red tape, financial constraints, political instability, and unpredictable supply chain disruptions. Each hurdle had the potential to delay or even derail their mission. Against all odds, it came to life.

Within the clinic walls, Omega led a small, dedicated team whose relationships with one another and their patients became the backbone of their work. People immediately showed up with needs—medical issues that had gone untreated for too long and diseases that should have been prevented but weren't. There were extreme cases of malaria, dengue fever, cholera, typhoid fever, hepatitis, and many more. Often there were not enough local resources to solve the problem as quickly as Omega would have liked.

Beyond Omega's expertise in medicine, he was deeply committed to the spiritual well-being of his staff. This was his ministry and his flock, and as the lead doctor, he was their shepherd. He started their day by reading Scripture and closed it with prayer, creating a culture of faith in the workplace. He chose to believe that Jesus proclaims His authority over life, sickness, and even death with an offer of eternal life to all those who believe in Him. In a place where diseases run rampant, faith in the One who saves is what made all the difference.

There was so much work to do, and all of it was good work. It would have been easy to run hard and fill every hour, to let the demands define the rhythm of their family life. But Omega knew better. He had seen what burnout could do to doctors, missionaries, pastors, and even parents. People who begin with clear-eyed devotion can end up numb, scattered, resentful, and exhausted.

Omega wasn't interested in becoming a martyr to his own ambition. He was interested in longevity, which required something more radical than hustle. It required rest.

So he made some decisions that raised eyebrows in a ministry culture, especially when busyness is often equated with faithfulness. He closed the clinic at four o'clock every day. He protected his weekends. He made space for dinner with his family each evening.

Of course, the community needs never stopped, patients didn't disappear, and their family calling was always present. But in Omega's mind, boundaries were the guardrails that kept him showing up with his compassion intact and his spirit unfractured.

At home, Julie had the same clarity. She wasn't interested in proving her worth by overextending herself. Living in a foreign country and raising four children is not an easy mission for any mom. In order to live the life of a medical missionary's wife, she intentionally chose to make her home life her ministry.

There were seasons when her work looked invisible to outsiders. Other spouses on the ground were leading or taking on visible roles, but Julie chose the mission of keeping the home. She chose laundry, meals, daily prayer, and reading Scripture with her children. Her ministry became giving Omega margin when the clinic days were extra hectic or emotionally draining. What looked like small choices of normal living were actually the scaffolding that held up their entire family.

In mission work, there can be pressure to prove your value by how tired you are, how many hours you've given, and how depleted you've become. But the Edwardses refused to wear exhaustion as a badge of honor. They had gone to Tanzania to serve, not lose themselves in the process.

It wasn't always easy to explain, and there were moments when they questioned themselves. *Were they doing enough? Should they be leading more? Pushing harder?*

But every time they asked those questions, they came back to the same place: peace. There was peace in the fact that their children laughed freely and felt seen by both parents in this new place. There was peace in the fact that their marriage hadn't been buried under their ministry. There was peace in the fact that they woke up with energy for the work ahead.

That peace shaped how they invited others in and how they modeled their leadership. They didn't attend every gathering. Theirs weren't always the loudest voices in the room. But when they showed up, they were always fully present. Over time, their steadiness and peace spoke louder than any hustle ever could. Other missionaries noticed and asked questions.

How are you not burned out?
How do you still like each other?
Why do your kids seem whole?

The Edwardses just told the truth—that faithfulness requires rest and peace. And they had come to Tanzania to be faithful.

TALL POPPY SYNDROME

In New Zealand, there is a well-known metaphor called the tall poppy syndrome: When one poppy flower grows taller than the rest, someone cuts it down. Julie Edwards knows this idea well and lives it out.

She isn't one to draw attention to herself. She's always behind the scenes and never above the work that needs to be done. She speaks carefully and prays consistently. When asked about her ministry, she's likely to shrink in frame and talk about the kids, maybe a few women she meets with, and the home she keeps grounded.

But Omega sees it for what it is. He knows she's a big part of the reason they're still standing strong.

Omega recalls a betrayal at their children's international school when he was asked to step down from a role he never sought on the school board but rather took out of a heart of service. The memory is steeped in hurt feelings and memorialized through broken relationships. The way it happened and the silence that followed led to a difficult season for their entire family.

There they were in Tanzania, serving the community in several ways, and the fallout from that situation knocked the wind out of them. But they didn't panic when it happened. They didn't stir up drama or offer quick-fix solutions. They did what they had always done. They stayed steady. They listened to each other, and when Omega needed to process his feelings, Julie didn't force a resolution. They prayed for each other when they had no words left. They remained in peace even though the situation was not peaceful.

When everything external felt unstable, their internal unity carried them through. In that hard season, their humility anchored their marriage, made space for Omega to lead, and allowed both of them to grieve, heal, and continue as a couple.

Omega and Julie went through that situation together. Julie's not the kind of woman who would ever call herself a tall poppy, but she has grown taller in Omega's life than she realizes.

BUILT TO LAST

Omega and Julie know their story is an anomaly among many families on the field today. That's why they were recently asked to share at a missionary training event. They didn't say anything flashy or necessarily profound; they simply told the truth and found they were met with an eagerness to multiply their approach. When they finished speaking, people approached them—not just a few, but dozens.

Missionaries, new and old, wanted to know about Julie's discipleship of their children and home, about Omega's boundaries for his medical work, and about their collective unity in the face of conflict and external difficulty.

They explained that going home to the States was never an option for them—and neither was changing spouses. They shared that a posture of unity is what had made their home solid. In an environment where so many were running on empty— missionaries pouring themselves out for others in the name of Jesus—the Edwardses showed up full, overflowing, and ready to fill others' cups.

Their story was attractive because of one thing: It was *healthy*.

Today, the Edwardses are serving as trainers for MedSend's Longevity Project. They were chosen because their marriage and way of life made people realize that *missionary life is possible.*

There's a temptation in ministry to measure success by visible impact, growth curves, or dramatic turnarounds. But the Edwardses offer a different kind of vision where a testimony is built on small, repeated choices to love, forgive, pray, wait, and stay.

Together they've become a picture of what long-haul ministry can look like when it's built to last.

MY TAKE: THE STRENGTH OF UNITY

Throughout history, God has consistently called men and women to step out in faith and trust Him completely even when the path forward is uncertain. Omega and Julie's story exemplifies that beautifully. Their willingness to trust God enough to move beyond their comfort zone and into a space filled with unknowns echoes the experiences of countless others who have walked similar paths before them.

Life in our broken world often leaves scars and is littered with disappointments. None of us escape untouched. Yet within the Edwardses' story—and many others like theirs—runs a golden thread of God's faithful love flowing powerfully across generations. This love is especially evident in families who consistently lean on God as their primary source of hope and strength. Yes, they encounter the pain and brokenness of the world, but their faith remains resilient and undiminished by trials. They know their Source is unwavering, even if their circumstances fluctuate.

What about you? Do you trust God enough to take the crucial first step to follow His call?

CHAPTER 14

SUSTAINED FOR THE JOURNEY

Relationships are at the very heart of God's calling. Not strategies. Not numbers. Not impressive results. Relationships. When I stepped into the role of pastor for that small, wounded congregation, I thought my previous ministry and business experience had prepared me for what I would face. I believed I had the tools, the training, and the stamina to serve faithfully. But I didn't understand the cost, and I didn't anticipate the impact it would have on my most precious relationships.

Though every story you've just read has its own details, the thread running through their stories and mine is surrender.

When I was pouring everything I had into pastoral work, I was convinced that perseverance equaled faithfulness. Meanwhile, Linda was withdrawing into herself, feeling more and more exposed and alone. I told myself I was serving God by pushing through. What I didn't realize was that I was sacrificing my closest relationship on the altar of ministry. And when I finally resigned from that church, it felt like failure. I wrestled with whether I had quit too soon or let God down.

But slowly I began to see that God was teaching me an even deeper form of surrender that put obedience to Him above the preservation of my image, my role, or even my own personal sense of calling.

It was messy and painful. And it changed me as a person.

That experience is why I can say to you with confidence that the health of your relationships is not a secondary concern in ministry. It's part of the calling itself.

YOU ARE NOT ALONE

If you remember only one message from this book, I want you to know this: You are not alone.

I mean that in a couple different ways. First, God never promised that following His call would be easy, but He did promise that His presence would be with us every step of the way. Whether you're just starting out, eager and open-hearted in your calling, or you've been serving for years and are a little grizzled around the edges, God is with you.

I know that sounds simplistic. I'm not trying to give you a pat answer. I'm reminding us all of a foundational truth from Scripture. As Moses charged the Israelites in Deuteronomy 31:6 (NIV) when they faced a transition into the unknown, "Be strong and courageous. Do not be afraid or terrified . . . for the Lord your God goes with you; He will never leave you nor forsake you."

If you find yourself asking impossible questions, questioning your next steps, or struggling with the relational realities in front of you, you can rely on God's faithful presence.

And secondly, you are not the only one. Your relationships and the specifics of your ministry situation are your own, but I promise you, you are not the first one to feel the way you do.

You are not a "failed missionary" if God asks you to adjust your plans to meet the needs of your family. You are in good company if you've struggled to see eye to eye with your teammates and had to trust God to reconcile what you couldn't on your own. You are not weak if you need to rest. In fact, rest was God's idea. Your marriage is not the only one that is challenging. Others have wrestled with grief and relied on God's sustaining love. You are not the only one to wonder what's next, question if you heard God correctly, or feel the weight of finishing well.

As the stories in this book illustrate, following God's call is not easy, but it's always transformational.

IF YOU ARE PREPARING TO GO

If you are preparing to go on the field, build a prayer team before you buy your plane ticket. In the early days of MedSend, we considered paying not only educational debt but offering full-support packages to help missionaries launch more quickly. After all, there is a desperate need for healthcare. People are literally dying without knowing Jesus. Wouldn't it make sense to get dedicated Christ-followers to the field as soon as possible?

But when I asked those who were currently serving if they would have wanted both their debt and their support goals met overnight, their answer surprised me. "Don't do that," they said. And then they went on to explain that as hard and humbling as it is, the process of raising support is spiritually formative.

Yes, it can be awkward. Yes, it's vulnerable, especially for highly trained professionals who are used to meeting goals and achieving success by their own efforts. But it's in the process of raising support that God knits together a team that will go with you into the spiritual battle.

Yes, you need financial support, but you need prayer warriors even more—your own Prayer and Care team. When you're in the thick of ministry facing challenges that can only be explained spiritually, you'll be deeply grateful you took the time to gather a group of people who are already on their knees for you.

Talk to those who have gone before you. Seek out those who have seen and experienced things, those who have fought spiritual battles and come out on the other side. Ask them questions. What do you wish you had known? What would you do differently? How have you seen God's faithfulness even in tough times?

Begin relational check-ins now with your spouse, children, close friends, and extended family. Yes, God is calling you, but the ripple effects on your relationships will be wide.

IF YOU ARE ALREADY ON THE FIELD

If you are already on the field, don't wait for a crisis to seek help. Relational strain rarely resolves itself. Small resentments, unspoken frustrations, and chronic exhaustion will eventually break something if they're left unaddressed. Take time to address those relationship issues early.

And that may mean seeking professional help. Do so without shame. The idea that we should be able to push through and fix things ourselves or that we need to carry the weight alone has worn out too many faithful Christ-followers. You don't need to wait until something breaks. The most resilient missionaries I know are the ones who raised their hand early and said, "We need help."

This is the heart behind the MedSend Longevity Project. I'm sure the program will continue to evolve, but so far it has proved to be a powerful encouragement to many. One recipient told me, "I don't know what our path would've looked like without it. When we might have burned out, we didn't." Another said, "This isn't just a blessing for me but also for my family and the people I serve."

The value of investing in your mental, emotional, and relational health can't be overstated. Ministry draws deeply from your soul, and if you don't seek out regular refreshment, you'll eventually find yourself pouring from an empty cup. So normalize "not being okay." Be honest with your spouse, your team, and your support network. You don't have to keep up the image that everything is fine.

Whether it's through the Longevity Project or on your own, build intentional rhythms of rest into your days and weeks before burnout ever knocks on the door. Do you have a rhythm of rest that truly restores you—not just a day off to catch up on emails or errands but time set apart to breathe, enjoy God, and be refilled by His presence? A weekly sabbath is a regular, embodied reminder that the world does not revolve around your effort. God Himself rested. And when we rest, we declare our trust that God is still at work even when we are not.

And then there's a sabbatical. Not every sending organization makes space for one, and not many missionaries feel they "deserve" one, but a sabbatical can be an amazing gift. It isn't the same as home assignment, which can be just as hectic in different ways as life on the field. What I'm talking about is dedicated time away to recalibrate and renew your faith and vision. Taking time for real rest may feel like stepping back, but more often than not, it's what actually allows you to stay in your ministry.

IF YOU ARE A SUPPORTER

If you are supporting missionaries, you are far more important than you know. When it comes to sustaining missionaries for the long haul, financial gifts are deeply appreciated, of course, but your prayers and intentional encouragement often carry the greater weight. You're not just a donor; you are truly part of the team.

Start by praying for the specific relational needs of the missionaries you support. Even as you pray for their work, pray for their marriage. Pray for their kids. Pray for their friendships and teammates. Those are the relationships that hold the work together, and often they're the first to suffer under stress.

Ask better questions. The next time you connect, instead of only asking about their work or the specifics of their life and ministry overseas, try asking about their heart. *What's been hard lately? How's your marriage? How can I pray for your kids?* A simple heartfelt question may open a door for someone to share a burden they've been carrying on their own.

And finally, provide tangible encouragement—a handwritten letter, a small care package, a retreat fund. These small gestures have an outsized impact. They tell your missionary friends they're not alone and that they are eternally valuable, not just for their service but simply because they belong to God.

FAITHFUL IN THE SMALL THINGS

I want to leave you with one final thought. Resist the urge to think that only big things count. Regardless of your position, real ministry is rarely grand. It's often hidden, unglamorous, and full of slow work that doesn't always yield immediate results. But small acts of faithfulness have long-term, Kingdom-sized impact. Faithfulness, even in the midst of difficulty or discouragement, can bear fruit far beyond what we can see.

When I was a pastor, I started a Wednesday night Bible study. In my small congregation, I was never sure how many would show up to events, and that study was no different. I had no idea how many would come. Ten? Maybe twenty? The first week, one person came. The second week—still one. But I kept studying, preparing, and showing up like a crowd was waiting. I taught that one man as if I were teaching a hundred.

When he and his girlfriend had started attending church, neither of them had a strong spiritual foundation. She had walked away from the faith. He had never set foot inside a church before. They chose our church because it was closest to where they lived. Nothing like being a pastor by proximity!

Week after week, we sat down together. We studied the Word. I answered questions. I listened. In my mind, the same refrain kept coming: Be faithful in the small things. Sure, it might have felt more gratifying to teach a full room, but the Lord impressed on me the need to be as faithful to one as I would be to many.

What I didn't know was that the man would eventually come to Christ. I would have the privilege of baptizing him, and he would go on to seminary. Today, he's a pastor who's making an incredible impact on the Kingdom.

I share this story not because it shows anything great about me. It's about a God who multiplies what we offer even when it feels small.

The small things are really the big ones in God's economy. They're the very things God uses to transform us to be more like Him. Maybe as you read these stories you felt like your struggles are too big and your offering too small. Take the bold step of surrendering all of it, both the big and the small.

As you finish this book, take time to reflect. And while you're at it, ask God to speak.

There is mystery in how God works, to be sure. But as you reflect, consider how God might be using these stories to change you. Find a quiet moment this week on a walk, during a commute, or before the busyness of the day begins, and ask Him, "What are You saying to me through these missionaries' lives?"

Listen for His voice, and let God's Spirit move you toward something, even if it's small. Reach out for help now, not later. Step toward healing. Begin again.

Live fully surrendered, trusting that God will sustain you in the calling. Yes, we are all broken, and, yes, relationships can be messy. But brokenness is not your identity. You are in Christ. And He makes all things new.

A BLESSING FROM ME

As you look up from these pages and contemplate the realities of your own life, remember this: The God who called you sees you.

He knows the weight you carry. He knows the relationships you treasure and the ones that feel fragile. He delights in your faithfulness—even in the unseen, ordinary, trying moments. You do not walk alone. The God who lovingly designed and knit you together and placed His call on your life will sustain you every step of the way.

May God give you resilience when the work feels heavy, courage when relationships feel strained, and grace when you stumble.

May you be strengthened to love well in every season.

May your marriage be a place of refuge and joy.

May your children know that they are cherished beyond measure.

May your teammates find in you a faithful friend, and may the people you serve see in you the patient, gracious love of Christ.

May your love for God grow deeper, and when you feel weary, may you hear His gentle invitation to come and rest in Him.

May your life be a living testimony of His faithfulness in the midst of every joy and every trial.

Go in His peace, walk in His strength, and live out His love in every relationship He's entrusted to you.

I'm for you. I'm with you. And I can't wait to one day hear the stories of transformation that came because of your surrendered heart.

AUTHOR'S NOTE

I am deeply grateful to those who shared their time and willingness to be transparent about both the challenges and the blessings of serving God in low-resource settings. Strong relationships require commitment and care even in the best of circumstances, and under pressure they can bend—or even break. These stories are not easy to tell, but the honesty of those who contributed makes this book valuable for others walking a similar relationship-testing journey.

ABOUT THE AUTHOR

Rick Allen is a leading expert on global healthcare delivery in low-resource environments. He is CEO of MedSend, a medical missions organization that has supported more than 900 healthcare professionals in 103 countries around the world. He is also the creator of The Longevity Project, an innovative MedSend program that protects and supports the professional, relational, and spiritual health of healthcare professionals serving in extreme conditions.

Under his leadership, MedSend has expanded in several ways. Today it offers scholarships to doctors in Asia and Africa for advanced training in surgery, pediatrics, OB/GYN, and several other specialties.

As chairman and cofounder of the Institute of Global Healthcare Missions (IGHM), Allen is focused on scaling physician and nurse training programs throughout Africa and Asia to build local capacity in mission hospitals.

Before serving at MedSend, Allen spent twenty-five years in the software and services industry and eight years as a pastor of a nondenominational church.

For more information about Rick Allen and MedSend, visit medsend.org.

ENDNOTES

1   Rob Hay, Valerie Lim, Detlef Blöcher, Jaap Ketelaar, and Sarah
    Hay, Eds., *Worth Keeping: Global Perspectives on Best Practice
    in Missionary Retention*, William Carey Library, 2007.

www.ingramcontent.com/pod-product-compliance
Lightning Source LLC
Chambersburg PA
CBHW070914130626
46555CB00001B/136

PRAISE FOR *SURRENDERED HEART*

Oh! How I empathize and resonate! As a former medical missionary myself, these biographies and Rick's analyses ring true! His insights crystalize the overwhelming issues faced by medical personnel who risk whole-life engagement abroad. He presents the raw stories, not sugar-coated; he asks the hard questions without forcing answers. His analysis of each couple's story affirms the positive; his interpretation is optimistic. The real issues, such as loss of self-esteem during language learning, are those I've seen as a counselor of medical missionaries for forty years. This book will inspire you and renew your appreciation of medical missionaries as heroes of the faith who are changing the world through living Christ's love in the world's forgotten places.

—DR. LOIS DODDS,
director, Heartstream Resources for Global Workers

So, you've heard and obeyed God's call to serve in medical missions, and it's clear He's orchestrated all the details. You just know you're at the right place at the right time ... and then that next thing happens. Interminable delays. Gut-wrenching losses. Inescapable work demands. Team conflicts. Forced expatriation. Or the reality that the work you came to do is now being done by others. *Surrendered Heart* chronicles those situations where the true, deeper victory of surrender is best learned. This is a good book. Read it before you go to the field. Then read it again when you've been there a while.

—BARNEY M. DAVIS, JR., MD,
Barnabas International

The real-life stories shared in this riveting book remind us of God's faithfulness when we obey His calling. *Surrendered Heart* will inspire, encourage, and guide all readers, whether called to serve or called to support those serving.

—**REBEKAH NAYLOR, MD,**
IMB emeritus missionary

Rick's ability to gently and authentically confront the reader with the often-unseen costs of serving in missions and ministry while maintaining hope and glorifying God is truly inspiring. Through Rick's personal story and the stories of medical missionaries around the world, *Surrendered Heart* provides insight into the impact that serving has on cherished relationships. Written from a place of grace and understanding, this book is a must-read for pastors, leaders, therapists, families, and anyone supporting missionaries or seriously considering work on the mission field.

—**DR. HILLARY WILDT,**
clinical psychologist